SPIRITUAL REALIS

SPIRITUAL REALISATION

INNER VALUES IN EVERYDAY LIFE

Communicated to
IVY NORTHAGE
by her spiritual guide
CHAN

Published by
The College of Psychic Studies
16 Queensberry Place, London SW7 2EB.

First published in 1988 by the Pelegrin
Trust in association with Pilgrim Books.

This edition published in 1995 by
The College of Psychic Studies
16 Queensberry Place, London, SW7 2EB

British Library Cataloguing-in-Publication Data
A catalogue record of this book
is available from The British Library
ISBN 0 903336 21 9

Printed and bound in Great Britain
by Whitstable Litho, Whitstable, Kent.

CONTENTS

FOREWORD

IN INTRODUCING to a wider public a selection of the spiritual teachings produced over many years by Mrs Ivy Northage in trance under the control of her teacher, Chan, the editors have endeavoured to present them in a form adapted very slightly to the written word in place of the original spoken word. In doing so, the greatest possible care has been taken to preserve the original meaning in a totally accurate way. Most of the changes, indeed, represent no more than a slight adjustment in the order of words within a sentence, and some sentences have been broken up into shorter ones.

It is hoped that the very practical spiritual purposes in these teachings, and the unassertive authority in the speaking of them, have been fully preserved in the form now presented.

CHAPTER ONE

SPIRITUAL REALISATION

SPIRITUALITY does not necessarily mean piety or any kind of religious aspiration. It is merely a clear definition of the separation of that part of your consciousness which is indestructible, and which will on the death of your physical body continue in another state of existence. This spirituality is the divine part of yourself. It is regulated to the level of your capacity to reach out to that spiritual rung of the ladder to which you belong. The term spirituality does not bring any kind of superiority with it other than that which has been duly and previously earned. Spiritual consciousness does, however, have access to levels of power and authority which, properly used, are superior to and can overcome the limitations of the physical world. It is in this display of authority that we are going to interest ourselves. We will try to explore one or two avenues of such superiority.

Everything that hampers you and obstructs you in life is directed towards your inability to cope. If you had enough money, enough time, good health, the right kind of education – every part of your discontent is prefaced by an if or a but, simply because these define your inadequacy in one form or another. So all the discord in your life can be reduced to this common denominator: inadequacy.

1

Now you may feel that this is an oversimplification. One is meant, surely to come to terms with life in one form or another, since this is what life is all about. We are told that by constant application of ourselves in the field of adversity and obstruction, we grow stronger. This is all very true. But how do we grow stronger in the process unless it is by acquiring some inner strength by which we can overcome the very thing which on the physical level would defeat us? So again we come back to this spiritual authority, which is our true identity, and which is superior to the limitation of the world around us.

Our source of unhappiness is very much an individual experience. What *you* may find difficult *I* may find easy. So we have with our difficulties an individual form of challenge, which is in complete accord with the spiritual objective which we have to achieve in this present physical life.

It is quite reasonable and logical, then, that as we come to examine this aspect of our experiences we become infinitely more individualised. Although the circumstances prevailing upon our varying problems may be very different, the basic principle of spiritual withdrawal to this reservoir of strength would operate in any of these circumstances. So whatever your difficulty, or mine, we are unanimous in that we each have our own particular spiritual reservoir upon which to draw.

Life is not accidental. Life is not something that is totally uncontrolled in terms of your influence upon it. You regulate your life. You bring about the conditions in life to which you are spiritually entitled, not as any form of punishment but rather to express to the uttermost the fullest spiritual strength with which to deal with those circumstances. It is a way of finding your own particular gift. Supposing you are very clever with your hands. Or perhaps you can compose music, or have the art of words.

When you wish to share your gift with someone you would try to compose, or make, or write something that would be an expression of your gift on the highest level. Now this is what life is doing to you. Life is your friend, and it knows your potential in spiritual terms, in that it is subservient to the spiritual influence. Life obeys your spiritual emanations. As you think in terms of positive inner strength, so you attract towards you the relative circumstances that will either express and beautify that about which you have thought or will, conversely, imprison the aspiration, because it is not sufficiently stimulated to break down the barrier or the density that life represents. This means that you have in your own hands the power to change your life if you should wish to do so.

Now I can hear you shrugging your shoulders and saying: 'I wish I could believe that.' I assure you that it is only a matter of degree. Everything you think, you can become. But like your most elaborate electrical circuit, it is obedient to law and procedure. You have to be very clear in your mind, therefore, of the basic order of such physical and spiritual reaction.

So let us come back to our spiritual realisation and this positive acknowledgment of its reality which says 'I am spirit here and now. And this body through which I function is a mechanism, a piece of equipment through which my spiritual purpose is able to operate. I accept, therefore, with that affirmation, that my authority to so regulate and direct my path, must come from within, and must be superior to the circumstances in life around me.' Again you would say that this is an over simplification. But, try as you will, you would very much like to believe it. Yet you have not been able to change your life one iota. I would suggest, however, that change for change's sake isn't enough. When we are thinking about spirituality and its influence upon life, we can't start at the end and work backwards. We have to come from within. If you accept survival, you must accept, also, a certain amount of personal identification. So in that sense, you are what you know of yourself now, but you are more than that. You have access to sources of power within yourself which, properly applied, can and will forge the path ahead for you. They will create conditions and opportunities that will be of themselves revealing, both in their objective and in their success.

This is not an accidental thing. Having accepted your spiritual identity, you must accept that to a certain degree life and its pattern has been preordained. It has been moulded to fit a certain spiritual objective. Because you are not able in your finite mind to witness it in its entirety, it will frequently seem to you incomplete, inconsequential, and quite often a series of tiny cul-de-sacs, rather than a clearly defined and continuing pathway. So with your declaration of spiritual awakening, there must also come the obedience to the directive that life provides.

'Ah, but' you will say, 'this is surely a contradiction. You told us that we could change our lives.' Yes, so you can. But change in the sense of objectivity. Change in the sense of positive proof, as it were, of your own advancement. And this again you will find demands constant resorting to this inner spiritual identity which you know as your inner self. It has different standards from earthly standards. It doesn't take any account of material difficulties. It has nothing whatsoever to do with inflation, with economic crises, with all the things that go to make up the structure of your cultural and commercial world, and the people with whom these matters are shared. That is, it doesn't take any account of ways and means. Only of objectivity. If you are meant to have that house, if you are meant to have that job, if you are meant to have enough money, then nothing can stop it except you. That's the way you can change it. But it does demand obedience to its own direction, which is, of course, where so many of us fall by the wayside, when we are trying to put it into effect.

Spiritual realisation, then, is accepting that there is a part of you that knows every inch of the way that you are going to travel, that recognises the cost it is going to be in physical and material terms, that has counted that cost in spiritual terms and is willing to pay for it. A part which will always recognise that, when life pushes really hard, the moment has come to retire inside and find the strength, the enlightenment, the guidance or whatever is necessary, from within. You may say that I keep talking about within. What exactly do I mean by that? I mean this recognition of superiority, this recognition that you wouldn't be confronted with this situation in life if you did not have the power within yourself to deal with it. A refusal to be defeated in any way. A refusal to make excuses for yourself, because with this spiritual supremacy no such excuses are necessary.

You see how it blocks up all our familiar holes of escape in terms of striving to find reasons for avoiding what we don't want to do? Now don't be distressed about this because life is intended to bring about abrasive experiences. If it was easy, there would not be any point in it. You would not need to be on this earth plane at all. You could merely learn a few things in the spirit world and go on from there. But there must be this positive abrasive, this positive conflict and choice, this way or that. And we are making these choices in ourselves countless times a day. It is, by this means, rubbing away the density and obstruction of life on the one hand, and cultivating spiritual supremacy on the other. So this reflects, then, in its basic superiority and authority in every aspect of our activity.

5

Now I know that most of you are interested in some form of spiritual service. First of all may I clearly define the difference between spiritual service, and psychic service. They are not superior one to the other. They are different forms of service. The spiritual service is the overall influence of your auric field, that contains everything you are and everything through which you have passed. Everything you have suffered, everything which you have been victorious over, is emanating from you. Your form of service is in sharing whom you are, what you have become, what you hope to be, with those who can come within your field of influence. You increase your range, and therefore your usefulness, by constantly renewing your inner self by prayer, by meditation, by any kind of concentration. And by a self-discipline that helps you to be aware always of the imperfections and impurities that are liable to contaminate this influence, to the detriment of those whom you would help.

When you seek to serve spiritually in this way, your very weaknesses are part of your compassionate understanding of the world around you. This does not mean you have to have a morbid concentration on your failings and your weaknesses. It means that you recognise that you have failed, and you try to find out if perhaps it is because of lack of strength and that you should have prayed more often. You should have recognised that your spirit was failing before it got to the point of irritation, retaliation, unkindness, thoughtlessness, and so on. But you don't dwell on the weakness as a weakness. Jesus, of course, came in divine purity and became part of an imperfect world. In doing that He decreased a great deal of the range of his brilliance in spiritual terms. He deliberately curtailed that which He really was, so that He might be accessible to those around Him. So in the spiritual sense, you do not need to dwell in any depth

6

upon your imperfections. Rather dwell upon your unhappiness. Dwell upon this because unhappiness will always come from inner discord, from something which is wrong with your spiritual unity with the divine. You don't say: 'I wish I had not said this or done that.' But rather: 'I said that because I was undernourished in a spiritual sense,and I must see to it that I don't allow myself to be so undernourished spiritually in the future.' You pray more, you meditate more, and the more you recognise your need and the more you strive to travel this spiritual path, the more dependent you become upon this spiritual renewal. You will find less support from the earth, and more and more from the spirit. This is what we call receiving directly the full measure of your spiritual power.

Now everyone has a responsibility, in spiritual terms, to reach out on their own behalf as a spiritual being. The psychic is using a gift, just as the musician or artist is using a gift, and all such gifts must be shared. The musician does not write his music and then never let anyone hear it. The painter does not paint his pictures and hide them away. He shows them, and people get joy and pleasure from them. By the same token, the psychic gift is directed towards a specific form of comfort and assistance. It is used rather in the way you use your radio or your television set, as a medium through which you can visualise, or hear things that are normally beyond your reach. The psychic will do this with the help of spiritual beings who are assisting in this procedure, which is quite simply transforming the frequency and emanations to that of the recipient. The medium is a channel through which this power flows. It is made accessible to people for their upliftment, for their healing, for their care in one form or another. So you see the medium is psychic, in the same way as you are musical, artistic, literate, or clever with your hands. And they should beautify that by doing all

7

they can to learn about their art, their psychic ability. I'm sure if you were artistic, musical, or literary people, you would learn all you could about the techniques of your artistry. You know it must have its own individuality, and you know that mediumship must have its own individuality. It beautifies and enhances this by a form of self discipline relative to its expression. The spirituality here is the degree, the quality of the psychic power. Just as, were you a painter or a musician, your spiritual quality would manifest through your art, although your art would be a separate example of spirituality.

This, then, is your distinction in the psychic sense. To be a psychic does not make you, in the pious sense of the word, a spiritual person. You are spiritually alive when you have recognised your spiritual identity. now for the degrees and levels of psychic aptitude. This is something, again, which is uninvited and unknown in many cases, as is the fact that you had any artistic or musical tendencies. There is always a longing to do that which you are able to do. You will say: 'That's nonsense. I've longed to do this or I've longed to do that.' Let me give you a little secret about that, which will help you in your frustration. If, perhaps, you have longed to be an artist, or a singer, but you have never had the opportunity to learn to express your gift. I am going to say unequivocally that if you really wanted to do something about it, nothing would stop you. So were you really the artist in the sense we know, or the musician in the way we know the old musicians operated, nothing would stop you. You would find a way. But you haven't found a way. You still have this hunger. Don't be at all distressed by this. Because, you see, it could well be that you have already been a musician, or a painter, or a dramatist, and you have used up that part of yourself. And when you hear the music, or see the picture, or watch the play, or read the book, you get homesick. The old feelings that you have already experienced awaken, and there is this peculiar ache, this longing for the past. I promise you that, nine times out of ten, those of you who say they have been so frustrated have already walked that way.

Spiritually, this part of you is only a tiny fragment of the whole of you. You are not expressing your whole spirituality, or your whole identity at this present time. You are expressing only that part which is relative to your needs. And, if you have already walked that way, this could be a liability to you. So if you can acknowledge 'just a little bit of homesickness, not frustration', then you can enjoy listening to other people, watching other people, reading other people, encouraging where you can, using this inner note. You may say: 'I can't paint myself but somehow I know when a thing is good.' Or: 'I can't write and yet I know somebody has found something.' You have it already; and here you can be of service and encouragement to somebody who is still walking that path. So you see, all these things have this one note, which we call harmony, in yourself. If you will find harmony in all you do in terms of spiritual exploration and investigation, then you are on the right pathway. You are at peace within yourself.

Now you see how important it becomes to have this clearly defined recognition of what you mean by the spiritual realisation of yourself. First of all, nothing can stop you except yourself. That is the first thing you have to say. If you find yourself longing for things that seem to be out of reach, ask whether this is really what you want to do in terms of service, or to afford you any kind of happiness, if that's the right word. I always think that is a difficult and elusive word to define. But if I emphasise harmony within yourself, you may say that you could never feel happy in your job, or in your circumstances.

9

Then I ask you to go within yourselves and look again at your own inner conviction. Because, you see, while you are quarrelling with life in any capacity, you are not going to recognise its true objective. By your very quarrelling, resentment and unwillingness to operate, you are denying your own progress through it. Far better to say that there must be something that God wants me to do, and the sooner I get on with it the better. Then bring your full faculty into it to enjoy what you do. If you don't enjoy what you do, ask yourself why you are doing it, because with a lot of you, your lives are cluttered. Your priorities are so terribly mixed. You must come back again to this harmony in yourself.

Applying this approach to the psychic field of spiritual service, let us consider the healer. Again, I am only generalising. Most of the healers whom I meet are dissatisfied with themselves. They tell me that they don't consider themselves to be worthy, or that they can't know of a certainty whether their healing is doing anybody any good. Or that they are not confident in the power itself as it flows from them. All these negative thoughts are intrusions upon harmony, because the spiritual force is quite infallible in the way it operates: if you allow it, it will operate for you precisely the way it is meant to operate, and all you are asked to do is to acknowledge it.

The fact that you have healing power means that the power is operating now, and nothing will stop it operating now. Your discontent can only impede the pure clear light as it flows from you. So instead of getting, we will say, a kind of laser beam which will go straight to the disability, it is broken up, so that the benefit received is made less effective by your dissatisfaction, not by any lack of healing power. Am I asking you to be complacent, then, and to be satisfied? Do I want you to say: 'Yes I'm a fine healer, I don't have to do anything about it.' Not at all.

Because life is busy taking care of all those things that spiritually you are capable of achieving, by refining and rubbing down those corners that would impede the length and the breadth of your particular healing emanations, you don't have to do anything about improving yourself, because life will show you the way by which you can grow stronger. And that brings us back to this dissatisfaction. 'If only,' you say 'I didn't have that sort of job, I could give all my time to healing. Why do the spirit people want me to work? Why don't they provide me with the conditions by which I can do so?' We come back to the discontent and disharmony. You *must* find obedience and harmony within yourself, the recognition of the perfect balanced approach to your spiritual usefulness.

Do we want you to become robots, then? Demanding nothing, registering nothing? Not at all. But we want you to know that there is only one important time, and that is *now*. You can't do anything at all about what happened yesterday. You can't do anything yet about what is going to happen tomorrow, because you don't know what it is. But you can do everything now. So we ask you, healers especially, to concentrate on the harmony which is now. You can't afford to lose your temper. You can't afford to allow yourself to become harassed, and upset. Learn to recognise your body's needs physically, so you get enough sleep and eat the right kind of food. You learn this by harmonising with yourself, letting yourself become accustomed to that which makes you feel well, makes you feel good, and at peace within yourself. And again you will recognise your own lack in these things, as you become irritated, jaded, and discouraged, with a sense of failure. What about those people who say: 'I don't know if my healing is doing any good.' You don't know if your healing is doing any good, because the person to whom you are sending

11

healing has a right to reject it, by refusing to recognise that something is wrong in their thinking.

Do you know what causes illness? What actually happens is that the spiritual part of yourself is out of alignment. Your body and your spirit are meant to function in perfect unity, and when you do anything, think, behave, act in any way contrary to this overall harmony, you bring about a displacement. Now very often this is recognised and put right, either by prayer, or by realising that a certain sort of food does not agree with you, or that you are not behaving in the right way to a certain person. But then there are those people who accumulate this sort of discord; people who say 'I will forgive but I will never forget; you've no idea what she did to me.' And they will recite it over and over again. This builds up a canker or a discord within, which is displacing more and more of the harmony. This can bring about all kinds of distortions that you know as illness. Seventy-five per cent of the ailments from which you suffer are brought about by persistent inner disharmony.

Now you, the healer, come along and you are suited to that particular patient and you restore temporarily this harmony, and your patient may say: 'I feel so much better – the pain has gone,' and then the next week that person will say: 'It lasted a couple of days and then it came back again.' If this is so, it is no reflection on your healing. You see, the person is doing exactly the same thing again, and so the process starts all over. There are some of you also who bear certain ailments and disabilities as part of your physical pathway. Don't let this in any way alarm you. Because when you have any kind of disability you either bring out the worst or the best in people around you. The person who is helpless through some form of sickness is frequently surrounded by people whom they refer to as

12

saints. You may be achieving something that without your helplessness would not be possible.

So there are certain spiritual reasons which could discourage the healer, in that he sees no lasting improvement. But again I would assure you that if your healing is compatible to that particular person, it is like carrying two heavy suitcases for them and giving them a rest. Yes, healing helps in all circumstances, but it doesn't always cure. You have to detach yourself from the results of what you do, and be content with the fact that you are doing this because your own spiritual awareness has taught you that this is what you want to do in order to make contribution by way of spiritual service.

Of course the same applies to comforting the bereaved; you can only relay what is given to you, you are not responsible for the level of communication. Constant self-searching is not something to be applauded or encouraged. I do, however, stress that there are many ways that you can and you should look to the equipment that you use in the psychic sense. We have already talked about the healer. But the medium who is giving proof of survival often feels that it is he or she who has given wonderful proof. Where you get this self-intrusion, then you get the same kind of blockage as the healer. You are the instrument of those who would communicate to those who would receive; other than that, you keep a clear channel for that which strives to penetrate.

Now one last word, if I may, about how you differentiate. How do you know, for instance, whether you are a comforter to the bereaved, or a healer, or a teacher? Come back to the longing, to what you want to do. Because, you see, everything you want to do demands sacrifice and self-renunciation, and I'm not just talking about psychic work. I'm talking about anything you want to do. In life, you have to sacrifice. If you want to be accomplished in anything you either have to train or study, and you have to sacrifice other things to devote yourself to that. For instance, you want to be a healer. The very fact that you want to be a healer is a very good foundation. Then I would ask you how do you react to listening to people's troubles? Are you the sort of person that they come and tell their troubles to without invitation? When you stand at the bus queue, or in a shop, does someone start telling you their life history and all the intimate details of their life without any encouragement from you? Then you are a healer. Are you one of those people who cannot bear to read about something tragic in the paper because you feel so helpless? Then transmute that helplessness into a clear light of love and compassion, visualise the person, or the group of persons, about whom you are concerned, feel that love go from you and you will know whether you are a healer by that inner warmth that I can only describe as a glow of serenity. This is very easy to find if you are a healer. Again, this healing covers a very wide field. It doesn't concern itself entirely with aches and pains. The healer can give you encouragement to have another go with that job; can tell you you are not a failure; that you're not a washout, you are somebody who matters. Have you met people like that? People who seem to give you fresh heart? These are the healers.

If you care about your fellow man, do something positively for him in terms of allowing your power to flow from you in this way. You will find that gradually this inner harmony will take on much more influence. You will say, for instance: 'I don't enjoy my cigarettes the way I used to,' or: 'I don't like drinking so much.' Nobody is talking about either of these things as immoral, simply that they will be reflected in this inner discipline. Before anybody gets indignant, I am not saying that the person who smokes or drinks should not heal. On the contrary.

14

But these are merely obvious examples. You will find yourself going against things that hitherto you enjoyed. It is no longer pleasant to do this or to do that. If you will aim constantly for this inner harmony within yourself, you will find it very easy to find expressions of proof of your own healing power. People will frequently say to you: 'I feel so much better for having talked to you.' You are a healer. You may belittle this and say that that is not very much. But I will again remind you that you are no measurer of the good that your power can do. The less you think about the good you can do and the more you think about the reasons for doing it, the more effective you will be.

For the psychic, of course, the results are more obvious. You see, or you have heard, even if it was a very long time ago. If you have heard, or seen once, then you have the potential, and you may cultivate it. But again you must want to do this, in that wanting is concerned with the care of the person to whom you are directing it. Why do you want to do it? If you want it for fame or for glory, then think again. There are many easier ways of getting that, especially in this age of mediocrity.

Then there is the person who is not sure about these things, although they have hunches, and know when things are going to happen. Or again, there is the vivid dreamer. All these gifts can be cultivated.

But everybody has a spiritual responsibility, or potential, in terms of being effectively useful in the sphere in which he lives. You do not have to be either psychic or a healer to give comfort. You can be spiritually and powerfully responsive in your own right. You can influence your own life, and in so doing, influence and improve the lives of those around you. Everything you are, you share.

CHAPTER TWO

THE LILIES OF THE FIELD

THE WORDS OF JESUS concerning the lilies of the field affirm how wasteful it is to worry about one's material well-being. This is an exercise in faith to allow life to provide for us just as it does for its creatures and its flowers. But I don't want to discuss that aspect tonight. I want to think about the lily of the field as an expression of God's love. I want us all to identify ourselves with the lily, the daffodil, the tulip, or any of the many hundreds of flowers there are. I am concerned that we should identify ourselves with the kind of flower that *we* are.

Have you ever thought about that? Have you ever considered that there is no one else quite like you in the world, that you are completely unique? We are told that every flower, no matter how many hundreds there are of its kind, is different in some small respect from the others. By recognising that this is true of the spirit, we can save ourselves all sorts of unhappiness, and unnecessary conflicts, and frustrations; because, you see, the kind of seed, the kind of flower we are is pre-ordained. I believe it is in the same chapter that Jesus goes on to say: 'Which of you, by taking thought, can add one cubit unto his stature.' By the same token, not one of us can change the kind of seed that we are.

Let's not think about our particular spiritual growth for the moment. Let's think about ourselves only as a particular kind of flower. If we can accept that we are unique, then we must accept our divinity, and the individual expression of that divinity. I am not suggesting that the kind of seed we are today is necessarily the kind of seed we are going to remain throughout eternity – this of course is another matter. We, at this present time on the earth plane, are passing through some specific physical experience, and have a particular function to perform. Now if we are healthy, whole seeds of our particular kind, we are going to bring forth good blooms. We are going to become the perfect lily that we have it within ourselves to be. But if we stray away from our own particular and individual path, if we constantly argue, and rebel against the kind of seed that we are, we are going to detract from the perfection of what we could become, and are, by our own acts, obstructing our growth. There is no doubt whatsoever that to carry out effectively the spiritual purpose that we have come here to fulfil, we must accept the kind of person, the kind of spiritual being, that we are.

Now you may ask: 'How do I know the kind of person that I am?' You don't. There are countless seeds that the layman could not identify – it takes a specialist to know and to understand them. The specialist in your case is God, who knows the kind of people that we are, and in His wisdom, recognises the right kind of soil and environment, and provides the right temperature, light, and moisture that is beneficial in our particular case.

Now you and I as seeds are as inanimate in this respect as the seeds of nature. We are dependent upon this spiritual law, this spiritual force, to provide us with the conditions by which we may grow, and if we use this same analogy, we may accept the soil, the temperature, the moisture and light as part of the pattern of the life in which we find ourselves. These circumstances which we so often rail against, the people that we complain about, the hardships, the humiliations, and the constant lack of harmony, the efforts we make which seem to be negative – these are all part of the conditions of our growth, if only we would allow ourselves to bow our heads and receive them.

To do this, we must have a clear understanding of the true purpose of that growth. If we are going to bow our heads in bitter resignation, as Job did so often, if we are going to say: 'I don't know why I have to suffer this, but there is no good complaining about it, so I might as well suffer in silence,' then we are like those who St Paul said were as sounding brass, or tinkling cymbals, in that we have no love, no purpose. We have no at-one-ment with this universal whole, that accepts everything in the light of divine perfection.

Let us take this to pieces. If you believe that you are spirit here and now, that you are divine, immediately you have acknowledged that you are a spirit functioning through a physical body. Then everything which hitherto seemed to be without purpose or conclusion, without proper order or understanding, takes on orderly lines of unfoldment. No longer do things happen out of the blue, like a sudden storm in its severity. Everything now has precision and accuracy within the scheme of this universal whole to which we all belong. But just as the lily of the field has to submit to the laws that govern its growth, so, acknowledging this divinity, we must accept the conditions the circumstances surrounding our particular species, and the means by which we are made to grow.

I wonder what the lily would answer if we were to ask it what purpose it served. We cannot eat them, we cannot use them in any utilitarian way – they are, as the poet put

18

it, a thing of beauty and a joy forever, and an expression of their own perfection. They are the visual expression of the perfect working of the laws of nature.

One philosopher once said: 'No man could look upon a rose and remain an atheist.' I believe that in their beauty they have done more to promote the reality of God than many of our teachers, evangelists, and philosophers of the past. There is a perfection in a flower that is an act of worship in its complete at-one-ment with what it was meant to be. There is a moment of revelation when you really look at each petal, with all its rhythmical perfection – this is the outcome of the small brown indistinguishable seed. So you see it isn't very far from acknowledging that the seemingly obstructive and abortive conditions in our lives, are the very conditions that cause us to produce the same perfection of unfoldment as the flower.

It isn't a very easy lesson to learn, because we tell ourselves there are all sorts of reasons why our particular experience is far removed from this mathematically precise spiritual law. How can we grow in spiritual purity when everything and every person around us is entirely antagonistic to our spiritual unfoldment? We can find all sorts of excuses – you don't need me to remind you of them. They are complete contradictions of the truth that we have found when we have declared ourselves convinced of the absolute truth of survival. If we are going to accept survival, we must accept this unity that ultimately produces perfection, however many aeons of time it may take. You and I within the framework of this unity, are perfection, however minutely expressed. That perfection can only be made to grow by our acknowledgment of the particular conditions supplied by life.

We are all individual seeds, and we each belong to a group that produces a certain kind of flower which is different from every other flower. The seed doesn't

19

change its particular kind of species – it just *is*. And this is what you and I have got to learn, just to be. We must make no effort to force ourselves into another group or family – we have only to accept. Now we can only accept by following the pattern of life, and if this pattern has brought us into a particular philosophy, and then seems to have thrust us right outside the warmth and comfort of its activities, we must not feel that our efforts have been rejected, and that we do not now belong within this spiritual truth and philosophy. It simply means that we are growing, and in our growth we are establishing our positive individuality, so accept the activity that accompanies that particular, different part of the family group.

This again, demands the same kind of obedience that every entry into spiritual service demands. It includes the people and the circumstances, the doors that have been closed in our faces against degrees of service that have hitherto been acceptable both to us and the people we have endeavoured to serve. It means we do not hit our heads against brick walls by continually asking why this has happened to us – wanting to do this or that has no place in the perfection of individual unfoldment. We are what we are, and by allowing life to show us the way, we provide ourselves with the conditions that will ultimately bring us to full and perfect unfoldment – the kind of people that we are meant to be.

In so doing, of course, we give back to God that part of ourselves that He has endowed us with, because we have used the experience of life to develop and grow. In another parable from the New Testament we are told: 'Where we had five talents, now we have ten.' So we give back to God twofold that with which we were endowed, in the first stages, in that tiny insignificant seed.

We can only do this if we obey the rules, just as the

plant must obey the rules. If you plant a flower out of season, it wouldn't grow, it would wait until the time was right for that particular kind of flower to grow and develop. So we too, quite often, have to wait for the right season. The seed is there, it is healthy, but it has to wait. Do we wait? No! We rush hither and thither, asking why things are not moving, why we are not being used. We have offered ourselves, but we have to wait – nothing can make things happen until the time is right. Not that there is anything wrong with us, but this is the kind of seed we are, and we have to wait for the circumstances that are productive to our individual growth.

Of course, we are not producing a single flower, we are producing a mass of flowers. Sometimes one flower is in advance of another – perhaps one has died off before the next has come into full flower. The one that has died off is one that we were very proud to identify ourselves with. We loved being with that group of people. We tell ourselves that they don't want us anymore, they've been very unkind and ungrateful. It is not that at all. That particular flower has used up what it had to give. This new flower is going to blossom along a different line of God's purpose and pattern, it's going to be viewed and appreciated and used by totally different people and circumstances. It is not quite ready, but it has a different influence, an influence that we must use wisely, because it has taken a certain amount of energy, power, and understanding to bring forth that beautiful flower, and extend it in the way it has been extended.

Now we get a breathing space – an interval of time between activities. We are not going to sit down and bemoan the fact that something beautiful has been taken from us – we have used it up. Just because it has died off in the physical sense does not cancel out the fact that we did produce that flower by our endeavours, our faithful

21

attendance to the demands that life has made upon us. But now there is an interval of waiting, and we are not a bit conversant with this aspect of growth, and are most unhappy. Here we are, struggling to acknowledge that there is something that we have to give, another link, creating a much richer promise of what we can become, and it does not materialise.

But if we will accept the reality of the circumstances and conditions which have been provided for our growth, we are going to learn to rest in these intervals, and allow the fallow periods to restore our strength, our faith and our confidence, so that when we obediently follow where this particular growth takes us, although we may be irritated on the surface by uncongenial surroundings and awkward people, inside we have the same tranquillity, the same serenity that the flowers must enjoy by simply being what they are meant to be.

So we can take this analogy step by step. It is not identified solely with one aspect or experience of service. It includes many such experiences and degrees of service. It can change constantly. But in all its changes and variations, it is as prolific in growth as the lilies of the field, because of its obedience to nature's laws, and the conditions provided for its growth. So too, you and I, inasmuch as we accept obediently the pattern of life, can become not one, but many flowers of the same lily that we are meant to be, each time acknowledging the beauty, the useful purpose of this particular experience, each season demanding, perhaps, a different productivity from us.

Taking the same analogy further, there could easily come into our lives a time of winter, where every leaf, every blossom, seems to have been stripped from us. But the gardener knows that every time he cuts away the old dead wood, when this precious plant grows it is going to produce even richer and more beautiful blooms. So God in His wisdom, directing your life and mine, sometimes painfully robs us of a branch, something that means everything in the world to us, and makes us feel that we cannot go on without it – we are cut, and we bleed. If we acknowledge the same wisdom pertaining to our growth, we are going to be so enriched by the experience, and we shall know that that which is now being produced is richer and more beautiful than ever it was before.

You must accept your life as a whole, you can't separate it and say that that bit is good and that bit is bad. This means, and perhaps this is one of the hardest things we have to do, that we must accept ourselves as we really are. We cannot endow ourselves with a greater and more fruitful growth than we are capable of at this particular time. You and I must accept the perhaps unpalatable fact that we are very behind what we consider we ought to be. But having accepted that, we have no need to feel discouraged or disheartened by it, all we do is to know that by our acknowledgment, life is providing us with circumstances and opportunities conducive to our growth at the level we ourselves occupy at this particular time. When we are ready for something seemingly more important, life will provide us with the opportunity.

Now how do we, having acknowledged this, find our way through life? Does this mean then, that we have no initiative? That we have no urge to be better blooms than we are? Does this mean that we just sit meekly back and allow life to dictate to us? It's not quite like that.

Have you ever really taken to pieces the things that make you unhappy? You tell yourself that you are misunderstood, you are lonely, or find yourself in uncongenial surroundings in your job. People are not kindly disposed towards you, people whom you have loved and trusted have let you down abominably, and, of course, you loved them so much that you have been very hurt by their behaviour. You tell yourself all sorts of things like this, and you believe them. But the fact of the matter is, you are unhappy because you are out of step with life.

Now suppose you acknowledge this particular unpleasantness, this particular frustration or abortive effort, not as something directed against and hurting you, the person, but rather the means by which you are going to grow. As soon as you dismiss the personal aspect from the circumstances, whilst you can still be saddened and made unhappy, you will not be so on your own behalf. As soon as you disassociate yourself from the personal element in those individuals who have brought about the hurt, then you see things in a much wider, clearer understanding and perspective.

If I may go back again to the New Testament, this is the essence of 'Father forgive them, for they know not what they do'. Jesus did not accept His treatment as a personal assault, He accepted it as part of His growth, His individual expression of His own flower, the kind of lily He was meant to become, brought about by the acts of those whom He sought to serve. But in His beauty, His perfect at-one-ment with the God force, of which He was so strongly and actively a part, He could appreciate the chasm between *His* understanding of the infinite love, and the understanding of those who sought to rob Him of this beauty and this divinity that He tried to share with them. It was not a personal assault, it was a rebellion against the light of purity and truth, which with His obedience, His humility, and His perfection, He was able to shine down upon the imperfection of those around Him.

In our small and humble way, every time you and I obey the laws of life, and say: 'If this was not necessary for my growth, it would not be here,' not with martyred resignation, but with an active participation in all that is demanded of us, applying ourselves lovingly, beautifully, to what there is for us to do, we are following His example.

Let us stop wishing and hoping, let's just be! Let's use each day as the flowers use the sun, the rain, the soil, the temperature. This is what I need for growth today, everything about today is going to bring me into fuller and more beautiful fruition. Let our prayer be quite simply: 'Give me the strength today Lord just to be, just to extend myself in growth with life meekly and harmoniously, in absolute accord.' And each night we will have produced yet another aspect of the individual perfection of the lily that we are meant to become. Let us put away all longing to be what we are spiritually both unsuited and incapable of becoming, but let us rejoice in what we are – not so much what we are now, but acknowledging, without any fear of contradiction, that we have it within ourselves to be the perfect specimen that we are meant to be. We can only do this by obeying the law, and the law can only be demonstrated and made clear to us by the pattern of life – this means the whole of life, on all levels of its experience. Go out to meet it secure in the knowledge that if we do it bravely and confidently, we must give back to God in multiple power and strength that with which we were endowed when we were sent here for this particular experience.

CHAPTER THREE

THE PURPOSE OF SUFFERING

SUFFERING is so much a part of this earthly existence, that to try to understand its place must surely help us to deal with it more effectively and patiently. What promotes suffering and why do apparently innocent people have to endure it, when on the surface there seems to be no reason for it?

Suffering is an essential part of spiritual growth. If this sounds as if it is an unnecessarily harsh part of earthly experience, and you find it difficult to equate it with an all loving God, just think for a moment. This God force is part of ourselves – we are not separate from God, this God power is manifesting through our present state of spiritual evolvement. This is why it is so important to have a basic conviction of survival, because without this, nothing else has any meaning. If you are doubtful as to the continuity of existence, if you are doubtful that there is anything to follow death, then you cannot have any proper concept of the true meaning or purpose of life itself, including suffering. This is important. So even if you are not fully convinced of survival, will you for this discussion accede that we, at least, have experienced that it is so? We know that we cannot die, and that there is an existence that is an instantaneous continuation, after you have left behind this physical envelope.

We can understand the significance and importance of this in relation to a hereafter. But it also has tremendous impact and importance in daily life, in that it provides meaning and purpose to that life. And since, as I have said, suffering is such an essential part of that existence, then suffering must have an explanation and purpose. You can accept your own divinity in the assurance of the continuity of life, in that the indestructible part of you is part of God, and you can translate that conviction upon many levels of interpretation and expression in your own personal experience.

This, now, is where truth has to give way to a certain amount of personal conjecture, in that within the confines of a physical body we are unaware of our own particular spiritual status. Externally there is nothing to show that the person beside you is any more spiritually advanced than you are yourself. Many degrees of spiritual evolvement are manifesting within a community or society, with no external signs to show that this is so. We can only, therefore, measure progress by the behaviour, or attitude of mind of the individual. We cannot always assess what is a good, or not so good, attribute, in that much is not obvious or apparent, especially in a cursory association. But if we pursue this line of thought, we would find that the people who are usually the most tolerant, the most compassionate, the most kindly disposed towards their neighbour, are, almost without exception, people who have had a great deal of personal suffering.

Now what do we mean by suffering? You would classify it as going through some sort of mental or physical pain, and, of course, you can site endless examples upon both levels. But what would cause you pain would perhaps leave some other person quite unmoved. We know of a certainty that on the purely physical level there are certain people who can endure pain much more easily than others. We talk about these people as being courageous, and, of course, to a certain extent this is true. But the people who feel pain much more acutely than others, are not necessarily less courageous because they feel it so acutely, and naturally complain more audibly. Neither are they less spiritually advanced; and this is why I say you cannot assess what kind of suffering each one of us has had to go through, and what sort of pressure has been placed upon us.

If you watch anything growing, it requires change – the seed bursts its skin and brings forth its particular root or branch, which in turn brings forth further changes to leaf, flower, and probably seed pod and fruit. Everything in progress, then, brings about a transmutation, which demands a certain amount of rejection. If you could relate that to physical pain, we have a very good analogy to ordinary spiritual growth. We know that as we grow older in physical terms, our physical body undergoes changes that quite frequently bring about pain – indeed the very entry into physical life itself is fraught with pain and difficulty. Now physical experience is a reflection of spiritual growth. Using this as an analogy, we can accept our time here upon the earth plane as a means by which we can increase our spiritual growth.

Spiritual growth is the hungering after God that has brought you here. You assuaged this in your spiritual consciousness, with its ability to penetrate your physical mind by supervision, direction, guidance, and subsequent growth. You have in your spiritual consciousness been shown the whole pattern of this your physical experience, and you have seen the changes, and the various rejections that have to take place to bring about this spiritual refinement. Spiritual refinement, or growth, is an increased ability to recognise and respond to the divine force of which we are all a part, and upon which we all depend.

This then is the basis for suffering. Suffering is the outcome of the refinement, or the growth. It is not an inevitable part of your growth that you should suffer, but in suffering you do grow thereby.

I want to go back to the early beginnings of your childhood. You will remember that as you grew in understanding, and people and situations became dear to you, you first felt pain. You cannot feel pain unless you love or care for that for which you are suffering. The people that can hurt you most are the people whom you love most, and those whom you desire to serve most.

Now immediately you will say to yourselves: 'What about physical illness, what about all the apparently wasted suffering in the world today?' But this is the outcome of man's inhumanity to man, which is why I don't want to get too involved with levels of suffering. If we can accept that suffering is the outcome of growth, irrespective of the kind of suffering it is, then we have a firm foundation upon which to build. Whatever degree of suffering you refer to, whether it be apparently purposeless, whether it be physical pain that is borne apparently for no reason, whatever the level, it is always the outcome of caring – this is important. You cannot suffer unless you care.

But if you don't know this with your physical mind, how can it become operative in terms of progress – how can this increase your spiritual capacity to grow? Here again unless you have this conviction of your own divinity, of your own eternal at-one-ment with the God force, you cannot understand how this can operate for you without knowledge at the earthly level of consciousness.

We have to accept then that there is a purpose that is divinely planned for you, and rooted in this earthly experience, and identified with the pattern of life that you are called upon to bear. The degree of suffering is minimised by this understanding. You can feel physical pain, but your pain can and will be alleviated by your complete obedience to what life is demanding of you. When you rebel, however justified you may feel in such rebellion, you are going against the purpose of your own pathway upon this earth plane, and your suffering is increased by that rebellion, because you are upsetting the harmony of your own spiritual purpose.

We suffer much more than we need – this is the real object of this discussion together. We increase our level of suffering tremendously. But there *are* levels of suffering that are inevitable, in the sense that they are the true purpose of our being here on the earth plane. So let me just very briefly take one or two examples of this in a purely spiritual sense.

I want first to take physical suffering, for example someone who suffers over many years with cancer, or some equally distressing and painful complaint. We know that this can be the outcome of resentment, of wrong thinking, wrong behaviour, and so on, and we can accept that. But let's ignore that side of it for the moment. Let us take the purely innocent person, someone who has no such resentment, who has nothing that justifies the level of suffering that they seem called upon to endure. What spiritual reason can there be?

Spiritually we are always striving to offer ourselves by way of sacrifice, which is again a part of suffering. What we are not able to see with our physical eyes, is the effect of the tremendous courage and fortitude with which this person bears his pain, and deals with the situation. This is part of his service to humanity, that goes out from him like a light, and those who are less strong, in spiritual terms, are supported and upheld by his example. Strength is infiltrated into their weakened frame by this dominant courage and fortitude.

That is one aspect, and it justifies this suffering, in this instance willingly borne, because the spirit is aware of the need for this particular experience, and the expression of endurance, by way of sharing the strength that it brings forth by this patient acceptance. But there is another aspect. In physical terms man is always trying to improve, to become more civilised, to understand the mistakes that his forefathers made, and to correct them. So yet another purpose of our innocent sufferer could be to offer himself, shall we say, as a guinea pig, whereby man is able to learn. This would justify in spiritual terms the need for suffering.

Now it is important to remember that without a basic spiritual foundation, the sure knowledge that because we cannot die we are here for a specific purpose, and that we definitely have something that we must fulfil while we are here, nothing has any true meaning. And sooner or later we are going to come up against unanswerable questions. So unless you have this basis of conviction, the explanations I have offered will be unacceptable to you. This earthly experience is an infinitesimal part of the spiritual whole. Unless you can measure your own growth in terms of eternity, of constant refinement and repetition, this present experience will loom out of all proportion, and you will lose sight of its true significance. You have always to come back to the fact that you are spirit here and now, and that important as this earthly experience appears to be now, when you have left this physical plane you will find yourself infinitely greater in a spiritual capacity. You will recognise that only a small part of you has been functioning in a physical body.

In the case I have exampled, only a highly evolved soul would be called upon to endure so selflessly this degree of pain for the purpose I have endeavoured to explain. But because they *were* highly evolved, and because they accepted the true spiritual purpose of the sacrificial service that this represented, they would have access to a reservoir of spiritual authority and power upon which they draw continuously, and from which their courage is both born and sustained. So the suffering as such is infinitely less than perhaps your conscious mind can accept or understand, not because it is not physically painful or severe, but because they are so supported and strengthened by this spiritual power that they are able to endure far more than you perhaps could, in similar circumstances. So you can't say that that person is being asked to bear more than they are capable of bearing, and that it is unjust because they have done nothing to deserve it, because you cannot judge.

Everything to do with spiritual attainment demands renunciation of one kind or another. You know yourselves that all the things that have happened to you which are vitally important in your lives, have contained certain sacrifices that you have had to make.

Let us take another aspect of suffering, the victim of the murderer, who has killed apparently sadistically, and seems to be cruel for cruelty's sake – what about the victims and their suffering? If suffering fits into the spiritual structure, there can be no aspects of it that we can't find an answer for.

Here again, you have to accept on trust that the spirit of the victim understands precisely what it is up against, and offers itself so that these people can have the opportunity to think again, and be less cruel and sadistic. In order that someone can overcome a fault within themselves, there often must be a victim by way of temptation.

If you find a person who is unable to accept suffering, and creates a certain amount of bitterness within themselves, this is obviously a distortion of the experience. We have free will and can do exactly what we like with our opportunities. We can bury the talent, or we can multiply it. The person who uses suffering wisely, therefore, is multiplying his talent. You know yourselves that the people who talk most about what they have to endure, and complain most bitterly about it, compare very unfavourably with those who have a great deal more to cope with, and complain less – these are obvious signs of spiritual acceptance or rejection. When people can't forget things that happened a long time ago, and keep talking about it, this is the kind of suffering that feeds on itself, and increases, if you give way to it. But if you examine the lives of those people who have gone through great suffering, you will find yourself admiring something of their quality, and you will find that they are people you can talk to, who can put themselves in your place, because they have walked that way.

Let us now talk about how we may minimise this suffering. We can accept that there is a certain amount that we have to pass through, because we know that it is part of our growth and evolvement. But how may we minimise this? Starting in purely physical terms, if you have any sort of physical pain, whether you have brought it on yourself by foolhardy behaviour or not, never fight pain, never struggle against it. Relax the body and let the pain sweep over you, accept it in love, and even if it is the outcome of your own foolish behaviour, it will very speedily pass through you. You will very quickly leave it behind if you give yourself to it.

Equally, don't resist life. When life demands certain sacrifices from you, don't struggle against it. Spiritual law demands that we obey the opportunities that life provides, confident that those opportunities are related to our spiritual purpose, and to the light that we are able to emit in consequence of this experience. The fact that we cannot see the result of our suffering means nothing, in the light of this positive assurance that everything we are and have achieved and attained, is being emitted from us all the time. As that experience, therefore, comes into our orbit and we do our best to obey its demand, we should not be in any way concerned with the way people behave to us; this can only increase our suffering.

This is, of course, illustrated in that most wonderfully comprehensive spiritual phrase in your Christian testimony, 'Father forgive them, for they know not what they do.' This is the apex, the summit of spiritual love. It accepts the suffering that is the outcome of the service, and refuses the pain of the rejection. This frees the perpetrator of the pain from the responsibility of having increased that suffering to you, as indeed it decreases your own suffering. Don't accept the additional pain of blaming the person who is responsible for your hurt. This again is a tall order, and is part of this growth that we are here to fulfil. But everything will be minimised by your acceptance that pain of itself is the outcome of growth at one level or another.

Even if part of our pain has been self-imposed, by our disobedience and rebellion, the very fact that we are bearing it patiently, and striving to release ourselves from reacting to those people who have contributed to that pain, must eradicate any previous mistakes that we have made. Either way, we are bearing patiently the results of our own imperfections, or we are bearing patiently and courageously the self-imposed service that spiritually we have undertaken to fulfil.

Now if we have this attitude of mind while we still have the pain to endure, it will bring about such a degree of serenity and inner harmony that we shall be constantly sustained and comforted, however intense the pain or the demand that the experience is making on us may be. This is surely the key to all kinds of suffering. Once you have accepted that suffering in any form is a privilege, and something that is an essential part of growth, and that by your acceptance, and the realisation that it is an example of your own discipleship, you will minimise its distress. You will increase your strength to deal with it, and you will find youselves infinitely more forbearing and compassionate with one another, because of the complete harmony that this particular acceptance and obedience provides for you.

One last word. You may be questioning my statement that only those who care can suffer. Now caring is part of your purpose here – you are in this earthly body because you care about your fellow men. Whether you know this or not, your spirit knows it. Remember that you are shown exactly the way that you have to travel, and what you have to give, before entering this physical experience – your spirit knows all this. It has a reservoir of power and strength upon which it can draw at all times up to its own level. Quite obviously, once your physical mind has become acquainted with this separate consciousness, you have access to far greater power, and far greater assistance than you could know without it. But whether you know this, or whether you don't, you are still here because you care, and every level of your suffering is equated with that.

Now if we could really apply this knowledge to our circumstances and conditions, by patiently accepting this basic spiritual principle of the purpose of life, I believe that a tremendous amount of spiritual strength would be poured into us, so that we could afford to be generous and forgiving, we could afford to ignore the hurt and the lack of appreciation, the ingratitude, the selfishness, and the greed, and, of course, the physical pain, which may be part of our burden also, and we could draw upon this inner strength, giving us a quiet serenity, and enabling us to rise above what is being demanded of us.

Maybe it would seem your path in life is fraught with loneliness. You will say that your suffering is in not finding the right companion, or associations, or you have people around you but circumstances deny you access to them. Accept with patience and fortitude that this is your intended pathway, and give yourself to it, and just as I have said in physical terms, let the pain and the circumstances sweep over you. Give yourself wholly to what life is demanding from you without hitting back, without striving to justify, and to teach people a lesson, as it were. I promise you that nobody can escape one iota of pain that they have caused another person – this is yet another aspect of suffering. We bring this upon ourselves, but we can't escape from it. You are only adding to your suffering by trying to form yourselves into judge and jury in any situation, however justified that may seem to be. So you don't have to worry about that. You can afford to stand back and insulate yourself with this inner strength, and know that if you are very hurt and sore, then by drawing on this inner reservoir of strength you will be healed much more quickly.

Much more importantly, you will be creating benefit from that suffering, so that, by your acceptance of it, it is able to shed its light and love upon those whom you have come here to serve.

CHAPTER FOUR

HOW TO REACT TO CRUELTY AND GREED

I WONDER IF you have really thought about this before. Usually when we are confronted with anything that is inharmonious or contrary to spiritual standards as we understand them, we tend to shrink away. We draw up our skirts from the vicinity. We don't want to be touched by it. It doesn't even occur to us that we do have some contribution to make in these situations.

I want to try to give you some idea of the contribution you can make to the eradication of both cruelty and greed, by your proper reaction to it. Your present reaction would, I am sure, be one of instantaneous repugnance and perhaps a justifiable anger. How is one then to react? Do we stand placidly by? Do we turn our face from it? Or do we do something about it?

Well now, in the first place, really to understand the position, you must be honest and register your own reaction as it is at the moment. It is useless for me to say that you should do this or that if you are not actually clear in your mind what you do now. You don't know whether this will be an improvement on what you already do. Just because you are told to do something different does not necessarily make it right for you, even though it may be right for the person who advises you. So try to assess your own reaction now.

Let us take these two aspects one at a time. Actually, they are allied. Greed very often creates cruelty, and cruelty very often creates greed. They are very interwoven. What, then, promotes greed, and subsequent cruelty? Or cruelty, and the subsequent greed?

Let us take greed first. Of course, it almost invariably arises from deprivation. You may say I am wrong here, because you know people who are thoroughly greedy, who have been deprived of nothing. I still say it is an outcome, a symptom of deprivation. They are either insecure in their level of love, or in their level of the necessities of life. So with that first acknowledgment, you are not immediately condemning, and turning your face away, you are acknowledging that something has caused this to happen. As soon as you acknowledge this, you are in a way making allowances for the outcome, or the expression of the deprivation.

To be able to understand this thoroughly, we would need to know the circumstances and conditions of every person who seems to impress us with their greediness and cruelty. Quite obviously we cannot go into the case history of every person we meet in these circumstances. But we can acknowledge instantaneously that they did not become this way by accident; that something has caused this to happen to them; that it is a degree of deprivation. Maybe it is self-deprivation, in that they have not gone about things in the right way. In which case, they have only themselves to blame, and they are making other people unhappy by their own ignorance and short-comings. But here again, we know perfectly well that, if they are ignorant, as they must be, to so deprive themselves in the spiritual sense, then that ignorance is something to be pitied, and not condemned. The first reaction, therefore, should be one of understanding as to the cause, which is instantly diagnosed as deprivation.

What about cruelty? Again, it is tied up with deprivation in that, in these circumstances, we always want to hit back. The person who has everything seems to arouse in us a greater degree of resentment, because we have, in our own opinion anyway, nothing. So you will find that all malice and spite, in fact all cruelty, springs from this same root of deprivation. It can be deprivation of love, that creates a hate towards society, making the person want to hit out and hurt everybody with whom he comes into contact. In acknowledging that this is caused by deprivation, therefore, you are not turning away, but are facing up to the fact that here is someone who is, in a sense, sick. You cannot have either cruelty or greed in a healthy mind or body. There is always something wrong.

Now there are many kinds of cruelty, and you would react to the degree of your ability to help. Let us take someone whom you know is ill-treating a child or an animal. While you can accept the instantaneous excuse of deprivation, your first responsibility is to help them to help themselves by removing the subject of their malicious intent. So that if there is anything you can do to spare the victim of cruelty in any sense of the word, then there is no question at all that you should take such steps as are available to you. Not, however, in righteous indignation, but rather so that the victim should be spared the effect of this sickness, from a person who is not responsible for his action.

I know you will tell me that there are calculatingly cruel people who think very deeply before they act. But I still maintain that it has its origin in some degree of deprivation and that is just as much a sickness as any disease.

So having done what you can to alleviate the victim,

you are still confronted with the sickness of the wrongdoer. What do you do about this? So much depends upon circumstances here, and I can only generalise for you. But I am trying to lay down certain basic things for you, that will give you something to do in any circumstances or conditions. There is always something you can do. We have been brought into contact with them for a reason. It is everyone's responsibility to make a positive reaction to any circumstances or conditions that are experienced by those on the earth plane.

If we are not able to see the person again, we can only commend them in love in our prayers, that whatever they are suffering from might be alleviated. Here our responsibility ends. But supposing we are dealing with some member of our own family, and their cruelty is more subtle, and not something that shows bruises at all, but a stinging type of mental attack. You have this very often in your own home. You do what you can to spare yourself from this, but you are constantly confronted by it. It is like a whip, it lashes you. How do you deal with it? This is something that is a very heavy cross to carry. There is nothing you can do physically. You cannot go to a magistrate and say you are being abused or treated badly, because there is nothing to show. Mental cruelty is a very difficult thing to prove. And just because people acknowledge and recognise it, it does not make it in any way easier to bear.

Again, I insist that it comes from deprivation. Maybe there is something in your own attitude that has promoted this? This is something that you must ask yourself. You must be honest with yourself about all these things. You cannot react upon a spiritual level unless you have got rid of any erroneous reaction that may, even in ignorance, exist within you. You must ask yourself whether this person has always behaved like this. Whether, if it is your husband, he was like this when you first married him. Or, if it is your father or your brother, has it been as long as you can remember?

It may be that they have been deeply hurt at some time in their life, and they are taking it out on all and sundry. But, whatever it is, it has its origin in something that excuses that person to themselves, and so we have to deal with the cause. When the cause is near to our own home we are much more likely to be able to find it, because the only answer to this kind of thing is a capacity for love. I know this sounds fantastic. How can you love a person who makes cutting remarks, who is always flicking the whip of their wit, and cruelly inflicting these smarting cuts to your pride? How can you love this person? And yet it is because they are deprived of this very love that they behave the way they do.

Now you must build armour around yourselves. You must refuse to accept the whiplash of this mental cruelty by insulating yourself, and acknowledging that it is not meant for you, the person, but is the outcome of the unhappiness that causes it. So you endeavour to build constantly a little wall around yourself. And, in return, you try to compensate, you try to create an atmosphere of love. I don't mean silly sentimental emotionalism that people often mistake for love, but the kind of love that God gives to all mankind, in that it is an unquestioning acceptance of man's integrity and his status. This person needs the care and love that is all around us, the love of prayer, the love of caring about what happens to them. This is why I say you must first examine your reaction, because our most common immediate reaction to this is to cast the person off. 'I've had enough,' you say. 'I will not stand it another moment. I will not put up with this kind of behaviour.' And by this reaction, you are adding to the already existing burden of their unhappiness.

We must accept that their cruelty is not done deliberately, but is the result of a sickness. We would not blame someone who yelled at us in delirium. We know very well that, as they are sick, they don't know what they are talking about. To a lesser degree, this is what happens to the person who is so unhappy that they lash out at all and sundry. This kind of cruelty can only be alleviated by a greater capacity for love, and a refusal to be hurt – that is important. You refuse to take offence and allow this to distress and upset you. If you can react in this way, you build a fortress of light around yourself, that is, in fact, the very essence of the love that the person is lacking.

This is the same kind of impersonal detachment that people very often complain about when they think about God. They say that God cares absolutely nothing for what is going on around Him, or for the children on the earth plane, in that He is totally unconcerned with what happens to them. But it is this very detachment that is the heart and the core of His love. For He is there for us whenever we are ready to go to Him, and will be immune to, and ignore all the imperfections, all the things that are unworthy, and all the things that are the result of our own sickness. It is only when we acknowledge the reality of His love, and our at-one-ment with Him, that we begin to realise the force, and full capacity of this detachment in loving.

And so it is with our relationships with each other. When we are dealing with someone who is deliberately cruel and unkind, we are dealing, if only we will allow ourselves to react in this way, with someone who is sick. And by ignoring the effect of the sickness, we are creating the condition whereby the sickness itself is alleviated, and is hoped to become cured. Sooner or later that person will be lulled into a sense of security. You know there is no satisfaction whatsoever in constantly whipping someone with your tongue if they refuse to rise or react. The only satisfaction is in knowing that you have hurt them. Refuse to be hurt because you have insulated yourself in this light. But you can only do this if you acknowledge that the person is sick. If you say that they are doing this deliberately to be unkind, you are reacting upon the same level. Unjust and unfair as this may sound, you are being equally cruel, in that you are reacting unkindly. Here is a person who, your spiritual knowledge tells you, is sick, and you are tormenting him further.

This sounds, perhaps, a little harsh, but it is true. Everything with spiritual knowledge is extra demanding, once we have accepted the reality of that knowledge. We must accept the responsibility of conforming to the standards that it demands from us. This means that we are brought into contact with various situations and experiences, so that we might be of service to each other. We are not considered, now, elementary enough to be allowed to cry about the way life treats us. We are disciples of a very powerful spiritual authority. As such we are given serious jobs of work to do, that include bringing us into contact with unpleasant people and situations, so that by our reaction we are able to alleviate and eradicate the darkness that they represent. Our reaction is a challenge, then, and we have a choice. We can turn our faces away, or we can accept the responsibility that the doctor accepts when the patient comes to him for help. He may not know immediately the exact treatment for that patient. But he will try this and that, and he does not in any way blame his patient for being there in the chair in front of him, and asking for his help.

With this cruelty and this greed we are in precisely the same position, in that we are being confronted with somebody who is sick to a certain spiritual level of

43

understanding. This can only respond to a spiritual alleviation that ignores what it does to me, and how it affects me, but that says: 'You must be very unhappy to be in this state. I must do my utmost to bring all the help to bear of which I am able.' You are not always able to do this verbally. In fact it is much better not to. Put it quietly in unity around yourself, to prevent the slings and arrows piercing and hurting you. And in that strength, a great capacity, a greater power of love, is going from you.

Now let us think more deeply about greed. Someone who overeats, for example, or is greedy for possessions, or praise, or a status in life. But greed is also something that evokes cruelty in order to effect the result of what is desired. For instance, if you have a position that I covet, and want very much, I can't get it by honourable means because you have done nothing whatever to warrant being displaced. So I do something that either makes you very unhappy or causes you to lose your temper. Or else I malign you and speak unkindly about you. I am doing this because I am greedy for your position. I don't think I can get anything relative to this upon my own merit, and so I try to oust you. But I can only oust you by being cruel to you in some form or another. Now you see the way these two are intertwined. I am greedy for your position, because I doubt my own ability and efficiency. I am deprived, then, from the inner self confidence that comes from knowing oneself, and acknowledging that there is no 'better' or 'worse', there is only the right place for the right person at the right time.

The person who eats too much is really the easiest person to help, in that it often arises from emotional unhappiness. They seek eating in this way as a consolation. I think we can rule that one out, because if we can find the unhappiness and deal with it, we can cure the person from overeating. No one really likes to be uncomfortable, and overeating does cause a great deal of discomfort. So the pain of the victim here is self imposed. It affects the person more than the people around him. One can be disgusted by it, but this is refusing to acknowledge its origin.

But let us look at the less obvious ways of greed. The person who is always anxious to deny the well earned status of another, saying that they are lucky to have friends in the right quarters, rather than that they have earned the right to that position, in that they are qualified to occupy it. The person who always tries to tear down those around him. The kind of greed that envies others their place, because of their inability to acknowledge that their own status is equally valuable. How do you react to this kind of greed?

If there is anything being done unjustly, the laws of society must be obeyed, because, far from making it worse for the unhappy person, this is helping them to be protected from further sickness. So if you see somebody stealing something, you do not turn a blind eye, you report it to the proper quarters. But things are not always as obvious as this. We are much more often in contact with the greedy person who is never satisfied, who always wants more from life.

So having acknowledged the sickness, do not stand silently by and allow anyone to be maligned. Say quietly that they have earned the right to that position, and nobody has the right to take it from them. You may not be in a position to talk like this, but you can think it. You can try to surround the one who maligns with auric light and love, that helps them to recognise the worthlessness of what they are taking from the other person. For it is only valuable to that person. As soon as it leaves the person to whom it belongs, it disintegrates, and is no longer valid and valuable.

You have to accept that this has been brought to your notice for a reason. If you are the recipient of either cruelty or greed, you are experiencing this because you have some contribution to make towards it. Refuse to allow yourself to become a party to its effect on you, inasmuch as you insulate yourself. I think the Old Testament stories of the men in the fiery furnace, and Daniel in the lion's den, emphasise this absolute protection from everything that is harmful to us, if we allow this capacity for love to surround us, so that we are truly immunised against the hurts. It doesn't mean that we will not feel them. But it does mean that they need not harm us, in the sense that we are in any way injured by them. Once we acknowledge this immunity, we are injecting a level of love into the situation that is the only cure for any kind of sickness, particularly those we are discussing. And, of course, an important factor in this is that, if we refuse to allow ourselves to be injured, the person who is inflicting the injury is not adding to the weight of the sin to which they are subscribing by this ignorant attitude of mind.

If you are not ready to accept this kind of immunisation and detachment that I have tried to advocate, don't be discouraged or alarmed. But do acknowledge the wrong of any self-righteous reaction. Don't try to justify yourself, in that it was a pretty abominable way to behave. Of course it was. But if someone breaks their leg, they cannot walk properly. They hobble. And this dreadful behaviour is a result of hobbling in a spiritual sense. It represents an illness that needs help and co-operation. If you are not ready to give them love, there is nothing you can do about it except to pray for greater strength. But don't be like the Pharisee, thanking God you are not as other men, which is what most of us do without truly understanding that we do it.

46

I think this is a very controversial and difficult subject. But I hope that I have given you a basic generalisation that will help you to understand a little more how important your individual reaction to any such situation is. I think this is something we don't stress sufficiently in our spiritual philosophy; that your thoughts, the way you react and behave, are being sent out into the ether. They touch the lives of those around you who are meant to be touched, because that is the plan of your particular experience. This includes the unpleasant side of life, just as surely as it includes all the joy and happiness. This, then, is the first question that you ask: 'How do I react at present to such things?' Then examine that, and see whether it is of any use whatsoever to the person and the subsequent victim. If you acknowledge that here is a sickness that you can do something about, then that will be so much more effective than self-righteous withdrawal.

CHAPTER FIVE

THE HIGHER SELF

I AM PARTICULARLY HAPPY to be able to share with you an understanding of your true identity – because that is what your higher self really is – your *true* identity. One of the greatest joys you have when you come into the spirit world is to see yourself as you really are – and most of you are completely surprised!

Let us define what we mean by the higher self. Your natural conclusion would be that it is your spiritual self and, of course, it *is* your spiritual self in the sense that it contains all that is good in you, but it is much more than that. It is a means of transcending the limitations of the earthly conditions around you, not necessarily by removing difficulties and problems, but rather by releasing your capacity, your power to deal with any and all such situations.

Your higher self, in the spiritual sense, is that part of you which cannot die and which, when the body itself dies, is separated from it, and becomes your spiritual form, your spiritual identity. In spiritual terms it is 'divine', the part of you which is indestructible. But we are dealing with the manifestation of this spiritual part of your consciousness through the limitation and density of an earthly body, an earthly experience and an earthly consciousness. There is an interpenetration, a kind of infiltration of all that is beautiful spiritually, that breaks down the density and obstructions in your physical consciousness and in your physical life. You use it as mind and consciousness because all your actions depend upon this. Without your mind, without your conscious behaviour, there can be no activity, no thought, no purpose in your physical life.

Your spirit, then, is a kind of divine energy that only has shape and form when it is released from the body. When it is incorporated within the body it becomes an overall source of energy that permeates all your activities. It is primarily your life force. Your physical body depends upon its manifestation. In a purely mechanical sense it is responsible for everything that motivates your body in its normal physical functions. Only by your conscious recognition and awareness of its potency can a greater authority be released so that your physical body and mind can respond to its greater power.

This, then, is your higher self. It calls for a conscious acknowledgment of the supremacy of your spiritual identity over the limitations of your earthly vehicle, the earthly mechanism through which it operates. But its release is very much dependent upon you and your recognition of all that you can become. This is the essence of the Spiritualistic philosophy; that everything depends upon the conviction of your own divinity, upon the conviction that you cannot die. Everything depends upon that, which is why Spiritualism makes it the foundation, the cornerstone of truth. But it is only the foundation. It is what that truth releases in you in terms of active participation that renders it significant. So the first release of the higher self is through your positive conviction that you are indestructible, that you cannot die. That part of you that is divine and will survive this earthly body is functioning now as a kind of liquid energy permeating all your activities. It has its own conscious intrusion and participation; it will respond instantaneously to any mental direction which you can send it that will increase its potency in any field.

How, I wonder, would you define the term 'spirituality'? I rather think you would lean towards piety. You would lean towards the constant resource of prayer and meditation, and, of course, it does involve these things, and I am not in any way deprecating their value. I am, however, saying that the spiritual part of your identity is the source of the energy to which we have referred, and that spiritual release requires the conscious acceptance and acknowledgment of its supremacy, its superiority over the limitations of earth.

By spiritual release you can defy the laws of gravity. By spiritual release you can defy all kinds of limitations that prevail in the world around you. Everything around you is solid because it vibrates at precisely the same rate, and its very solidity is its limitation. But with spiritual release into your physical function you can vary your vibration, you can lift your frequency so that you are in receipt of levels of thought, of consciousness, of hearing, and of sight that are way beyond the limitations of the physical world in which your body operates. These are positive statements of fact. They are assurances that you, as a spiritual being, can overcome all kinds of limitations by resorting to your higher self.

I want now to try to convince you of your own potential within this framework of limitation and ascendancy.

Everything in your physical life is geared to a spiritual purpose. You do not understand this with your physical mind because it is not able to accept the wider expanse of spiritual issues. But, in spiritual terms, you have come here on earth to establish a refinement. We call it a 'refinement' because the experiences that life provides bring a purification of your spiritual consciousness; your higher self becomes purified. Through its power over the density of earth it releases its own dross, thereby drawing nearer to the divine light of perfection.

All the intricate purpose of that refinement is contained in the many experiences of life through which you pass, none of which are meant to be insurmountable – all of which are created and fashioned so that you might resort to this inner reservoir of power.

You also have a measure of spiritual energy which functions on a fairly superficial level. This is not in any way derogatory; it is again a statement of fact. Everything you are and everything you do without due thought or concentration is the outcome of this superficial spiritual energy, still due to your higher self but not higher in the sense in which we are dealing with it now. Everything about you responds to this superficial level. But with persistent positive assurance of a power within you that can overcome any problem, with positive resort to your higher self upon all levels of experience, you are able to refine its awareness, its power of penetration and perception, that it not only exercises its superficial source of energy, but also begins to bring into play its deeper resources, its reservoirs of strength.

Every incarnation is like a facet of a diamond. It is individual in itself but it beautifies the whole. You are all in various stages of development and have certain facets of your diamond that are completed. Some of you are able to remember past experiences; some of you have no such recollection. Recollection is only useful if it is an asset to your present development. Many of you are confused about this because you feel that a high proportion of the circumstances, the conditions and the demands that are made upon you in this life are the result

51

of bad behaviour in a previous life. It is not quite like that, although there must be an element of this. The purpose of life is to increase refinement, and quite obviously if one has not made a very good job of the refinement process in a previous life the overall quality of the present life must, to a certain extent, be marked. But it is not more than that. You are not paying the price of misdemeanours, mistakes or 'sins' of the past incarnation. You are, however, dealing with overall weaknesses which prevailed in that previous incarnation; your incarnations are not concerned with detail but with the essence, the spiritual energy that has been withdrawn from the experience on death and has gone to the make up of the whole of your diamond. In this sense every life is separate in itself, but it does contain the essence, the overall quality of previous incarnations. If you picture each life as being an essence that is poured into a bottle, and the whole bottle of essence as a reservoir, this present incarnation has a thread which can, as needed, draw on the essence to bring greater strength and greater power to the present flow of spiritual energy.

The more that you are able to acknowledge the reality of this higher self and its powerful supremacy over the limitations of life, the more it is forced (because its present energy is somewhat superficial) to seek its reservoir of strength. This reservoir of strength is not just more energy; it is related to the spiritual experiences from which you are now permanently released, the essence of which may contain the things you wish you had been able to overcome in previous incarnations. This brings an imperfection into the essence which initiates the process of refinement in this and subsequent incarnations. The details of occurrences in previous lives are now quite irrelevant; the imperfection will be refined in an appropriate field of physical experience. It is only the superficial part of your energy that is concerned with physical detail and physical experience. The thread that is tapping the reservoir of energy is able to reach out to those aspects of light and power to which it is heir in the spiritual state, aspects which are far above those which can be acquired in physical activity in the present incarnation.

So not only are you able to draw upon the energy itself, you are also able to tap spiritual sources of thought, of instruction, and of counsel and to draw them into yourself. This doesn't come in conscious thoughts like: 'do this', 'do that', 'don't do that', 'go there' or 'don't go there'. It comes and it beautifies the overall spiritual energy and intensifies its capacity to influence your physical and material behaviour. You can exercise it on your own behalf with complete confidence, with absolutely no doubt whatever of the outcome.

Let us now try to bring these ideas into the focus of experience. Perhaps you feel that hunches and intuition are dependent upon psychic activity, but psychic activity is something different. It contains the same spiritual energy – everything does, nothing is separate from that – but it contains no more than is demonstrated by a skilled carpenter or a highly gifted musician or dramatist. You all have spiritual energy; psychic energy comes into the field of experience and into spiritual energising. Do not confuse awareness and intuition with psychic ability. The two are quite different, though they are recognised in much the same way.

Intuition and awareness are the result of the infiltration of the higher self. Another way of describing this would be 'conscience'. You may feel uneasy about a particular kind of behaviour; perhaps you don't like yourself for doing this or perhaps you wish you hadn't done or said that. These are infiltrations of the higher self. Everything to do with your physical consciousness is emotive. You feel comfortable or uncomfortable, you feel happy or unhappy; everything to do with your physical consciousness responds with feeling. So the intrusion of the higher self has to be expressed physically through feeling. When you don't like yourself for doing this, when you wish you hadn't done that, when you feel that it was a mistake – here we have the higher self beginning to dominate, or trying to dominate the physical.

Everything that happens in your life is responsive to the note that this spiritual self, this higher self, is emitting. You send out a sound, you send out a light, you send out a colour, and all of these influence actions and behaviour in the world around you. Life is compelled to respond to that note, and in this way everything that happens to you is related to the process of refinement. It is brought about by spiritual authority, by spiritual demand, which is encompassed in the spiritual or higher self from which emanates the light, the colour, and the power; and life must respond.

It is important to have a positive foundation upon which to build. You must be sure of your spiritual identity, you must be sure of your own divine indestructibility, you must be sure of yourself as a part of the spiritual consciousness that is pervading and controlling the physical envelope in which you operate. It is important to build your foundations upon a rock. Spiritual philosophy without such foundations will stand you in very little stead. This higher self does not necessarily bring advantage in itself; indeed, many of you, when talking about its intrusion into your conscience, wish very much that it did not have such a loud voice, that it did not make you feel so uncomfortable. 'It's no good', you say, 'I can't do it; I know everyone else does it and they seem to get away with it, but I can't.' Of course you can't, because your spiritual power, your higher self, is too authoritative. So let us accept the reality, the function and the means of working of the higher self and let us pinpoint it and focus it upon the earth and in the world around us.

Quite obviously I can't detail specific things that have happened in your life with accuracy, but in the main the things that cause you the greatest unhappiness are those that challenge the intrusion of the self. The things that make you most unhappy are usually those that cause you to feel that you are being denied something that seems quite reasonable to the 'I'. Perhaps you want love and affection from someone who seems to be apathetic or indifferent. Perhaps you want a fair day's wage for a fair day's work; you don't mind working for it but you feel you are being exploited. Notice that all the challenges seem to be directed at the way *you* feel, the way *you* ought to be treated, the way *you* ought to be considered. Take the problems that are uppermost in your mind and you will find that the *I* is foremost, in the pain or discomfort that they afford you or perhaps in anger if you feel that you are being treated unjustly. But it all comes back to *you*.

So you can see that everything in life is geared, on the one hand in its density, to put *you* in the forefront, while on the other hand the spiritual side is saying: 'You should forget yourself, you should want to understand' – or in those beautiful words of St Francis: 'To understand rather than to be understood, to love rather than to be loved.' Here the higher self is wanting to put down the 'you', the 'ego', not because there is anything wrong with being happy, not that there is anything wrong with being fair and just, but rather that this is the only way that density, the lower part of your consciousness, can make any kind of challenge to the higher self; and there must be challenge, there must be conflict, there must be a choice, otherwise there is no demand to exercise your higher level of consciousness and authority in the world around you.

So what are you to do? Do you just suffer injustice? Do you just bear with apathy and indifference, although you are pouring out your heart in love and consideration? Here again you have to act according to your own level of spiritual influence because the higher self will always demand the note of truth. The higher self will not accept into itself: 'I ought, I must, I should.' It will only accept: 'I want to love more than to be loved – I want to understand more than to be understood', and so on. It will not accept the 'oughts' or the 'musts' or the 'shoulds'. Everything to do with the higher self operates on the pure, divine note of love; not the silly sentimental love that you feel emotionally, but an overriding love that is synchronised into that most beautiful of all statements: 'Father, forgive them, for they know not what they do.' Surely the purity of self-renouncing love is enshrined in that sentence; and that is the only spiritually acceptable level of love.

You must not let this defeat you. I can almost hear you saying: 'This is an aspiration that I could not possibly achieve.' But you can achieve it. Remember that life is geared to your spiritual note. It cannot demand from you more than you are able to give. It will, of course, pile its pressures and its burdens upon you to a degree that will force you to seek the reservoir of strength and power. It will sometimes so obliterate the brightness of the light that you feel totally devoid of it. If there are times when you feel that you have nothing left in which you can believe, that you have nothing more to work for, and that you have no sense of purpose, these are the little victories of the denser side of your nature and the very essence of the conflict and challenge that purification represents. But if you resort to prayer and to meditation, with a positive acknowledgment that nothing can happen to

56

you in life which you have not the power to overcome, then nothing can be demanded of you that you have not the power within yourself to deal with. Acknowledging this, even though you are bound down with the sense of your own failure, releases the power to you, even while you are being crucified, and it will bring you the strength to release the higher self into your consciousness.

Let us deal with this in a more practical way, which will help you with any situation over which you feel you have no control. There is *nothing* that is beyond your capacity – and I mean nothing – from the smallest detail to the greatest aspiration. You cannot aspire to anything that you cannot achieve. If you do not think of it, then quite obviously you cannot achieve it, but if you do think of it, whatever it may be, you have the power within yourself to achieve it, because you would not think of it if it were not within the framework of your pattern, your physical nature. You may think that I am making this sound too fatalistic; that there is a kind of inevitability about life. To a certain degree, within the framework of your capacity, this is so, but there are countless opportunities to bring about the process of purification, so that although you may fail in one thing or turn your back upon another, there are many, many other opportunities. Think of different roads leading to a town; there are many, many ways and if you don't go one way you can go another. Life can vary to provide you with alternative opportunities in the particular direction demanded. Don't be too confused or pressed down by detail; detail is quite irrelevant. It is what the experience brings forth from you that matters rather than the experience itself. So don't get too bogged down with the things that are happening to you, but think of the effect that they are having on you. Are they making you stronger? Are they making you feel more confident? Are they making you feel discouraged? Are you allowing the darker side to overcome you or are you allowing the challenge to increase your capacity? Always, always, spirit will multiply its own energising in the field of illumination and counsel.

I am making it sound too easy, and, of course, it is not easy. But it is practical advice and I promise you that if you will concern yourself with what you consider to be your job, regardless of what direction it is in, you have a perfect right to choose your own priorities. You have a perfect right to decide for yourself what you consider to be most important and if, having carefully chosen, you want to do one thing more than another, then that becomes attuned to your higher self. There is no right and wrong, only a requirement for complete self-honesty. It is no use saying: 'I ought to do this but I don't want to do it.' That is doing it without love. As St Paul said: 'It is empty, it is void'; it achieves nothing and you will have the same thing to deal with again until you offer your heart in its execution. I am not asking you to sentimentalise or to feel this loving, flowing spiritual power in everything you do; I am, however, asking you to be absolutely honest with yourself, and that when you consider your own behaviour you will try to do the thing that feels most acceptable to you in terms of inner serenity and inner peace.

I talked earlier about your conscience. There are certain things of which you say: 'It would be much easier to do that but I couldn't sleep at night if I did it.' When there is no doubt in your mind about your choice you are giving in love, you are giving with the higher self. But because life is a challenge, because the whole process is one of purification and refinement, there must also be levels of indecision, of doubt, and of confusion. So don't worry about the details; don't worry whether you have done this correctly or whether you have done that incorrectly, but just say to yourself: 'How do I *feel* about it?' Pray about it if you are in doubt, and then get on with what is nearest to you and to the doubt. Most of the dissipation of the power and authority of the higher self is brought about by looking for tomorrow's demands or next week's demands, next month's demands or next year's demands. If you can say: 'I don't know how I am going to manage so-and-so but I *can* get on with this', and if you can identify yourself wholly with the release of spiritual energy to achieve its perfection, you will find that by your very obedience, by your very response to that spiritual force you have increased your capacity, and by the time the matter about which you are feeling concerned is ready to be tackled, you will have the knowledge, the understanding, and the enlightenment to deal with it. How does it work, then? It isn't usually a little voice coming into your head saying: 'Do this, do that', although on occasion that does occur. It is an overall distribution which improves and increases your capacity on all levels of consciousness, not just in respect of that about which you are anxious, but in respect of everything else as well. By your application to your higher self everything about you is increased in purity and refinement, so that everything you do will be improved by resorting to the inner light, to inner direction, and counsel. Don't be in the least dismayed when dark days overtake you because, as I have said, if you will refuse to allow yourself to be dissuaded against victory – even though you feel badly about it – you will be stimulating your higher self to a greater level of power and efficiency.

One cannot change truth. We could talk about these matters on different levels and from different aspects, but if you are meant to have a particular job, if you are meant to have a particular house, if you are meant to go in a particular way, then nothing can stop you. But if you are perpetually frustrated in a particular direction, if a door repeatedly closes upon you, why not reconsider, why not resort again to the higher self? It is perhaps the physical part of yourself that is blinding you to the inner direction, to the inner power which would steer you into another road, another possibility? Perhaps it is not that particular door that you are required to open, in spiritual terms; its very closing may be a spiritual effort to protect you and guard you against futility and subsequent sorrow at your waste of effort. If you come back to the problem later, there is a part of you that knows the way; there is a part of you that understand exactly why it has to be. Even if your consciousness cannot absorb it at a particular time, because you are too unhappy or too confused or too hurt, never mind – try to acknowledge that somewhere there is an answer and then bring all the strength you can bear upon what is to be done now.

It may have surprised you that I have not gone into the meditative process of releasing the higher self so, very briefly, I am going to tell you what that accomplishes. It is a good thing, as prayer is a good thing, but all it does is to increase your energising capacity; it brings back to your body a greater degree of your internal energy. It doesn't make you a better person but it can bring a greater vitality in spiritual terms, so that the physical consciousness is more challenged, is more in conflict with the world around you. That is why you feel so often when you have been in meditation and in prayer that you are brought back to earth with a bump. Of course you are, because the energy has to infiltrate, it has to penetrate, and its penetration breaks down the density. It cannot achieve anything by itself; your higher self is the energising force that will break down all the challenging limitations of the world around you that cause you to say: 'I can't do that – I can go on no longer – I don't want to do that.' The higher self can break down all that negativity, and it does. But it has to have your conscious participation. So you start by acknowleding its reality, you go on to acknowledge its function in terms of energy and influence, and then you accept its supremacy over the conditions of life around you. I promise you that if you apply this to the greatest or the least of your experiences you will not need to come to a lecture about the higher self; you will be able to lecture on it yourselves.

CHAPTER SIX

THE NOTE OF TRUTH

I WANT TO EXPLORE what we mean by truth, or reality. You are told certain facts, and because they satisfy a responsive part of your consciousness, you accept them as truth. But as you grow in understanding, things that have previously satisfied that part of your consciousness no longer do so. You now have a different concept of that which seemed so acceptable; you find yourselves being fraught with confusion over something that you used to accept with confidence.

This is inevitable in any sort of spiritual growth. But how do we know, when we accept these things and take them within ourselves in this half knowledge of their authenticity, that we are not building for ourselves obstructions and difficulties that will make it awkward for us to rid ourselves of them in the future? How can we be sure that as we explore the pathway of truth, the things we absorb can be transmuted to a wider canvas without being contradicted by that transmutation?

Before we can really go into this very profound subject we must examine our own purposes and motives, and ask ourselves if we are absolutely sincere in our efforts to explore and understand truth. For instance, you may feel that you want to know more about the spirit world, not because you are interested in those who inhabit that world, but rather that you wish to have an edge over others by the extension of knowledge that you can obtain. This motive, human and acceptable on the level to which it belongs, would not enhance your efforts to explore and understand truth, although truth would be necessary in your experiencing of the extension of your consciousness. So before we dismiss these half truths as trivial we must consider our own worthiness or unworthiness to receive anything better. I want you to recognise that everything you feel impelled to explore, however trivial or unimportant it may appear to be, must have this inner core of desire for truth.

Quite often when you believe sincerely that you are seeking truth you are deceiving yourself, in that when you are given truth you fail to recognise it. So how can we know and understand this inner reality, this inner truth?

If you have explored spiritual truths and philosophy you will have discovered in yourselves an extension of your normal consciousness. You have an awareness beyond the limitations of your five senses and that gives you what we shall call a note, an inner note of responsive reality and truth. If you will listen inside yourself, every experience, whether trivial or important, will have a responsive note. We often recognise the kind of people we feel at home with; we can meet someone for the very first time and feel that we have known them all our life. This is the note of truth, responsive and reciprocated, and our certain awareness of at-one-ment with this person is the harmonising of the note of truth. Everything that we seek by way of guidance, inspiration, and extension of our knowledge must have this responsive note. While you are listening to me you may not agree with what I am saying, but you will feel the integrity and sincerity of the effort behind it. It is quite another matter that your mind, your intellect, cannot always accept what you listen to.

Oddly enough we are reluctant to cultivate this awareness because once we do so we have no escape; we cannot turn a deaf ear nor a blind eye to what it demands of us. We say that we feel inside ourselves that something is right or wrong; this is our voice of truth. If we listen to it, it gives us clear directions, but we confuse it by involving our personal desires. 'We only want to do that which is right', we say with our lips, but 'right' has to agree with what we have already made up our minds to do or with what we want to happen to us. Of course these are human failings, but there are many things that we could do to strengthen this inner reality that would make no really drastic demands upon our obedience. If we could be really honest in ourselves in small details we should so cultivate our integrity that it would be much more distinctive and powerful when it came to the wider issues.

I do not mean to infer from this that we have to be brutal to one another because of the need for truth. That would not be truth; if you could examine the note behind that kind of behaviour you would very often find a definite desire to hurt or to hit back. Truth is much more spiritually aware than that; it expresses itself by rejection of anything that is false. It does not have to voice that rejection; it can, by its own withdrawal, remove itself from the contamination of anything hypocritical, tawdry or false in complete obedience to that inner note. It need not commit discourtesy in the process, in the conventional sense of the term. It is inevitable that it will create resentment, in that the light that shines out from this kind of integrity always creates discomfort in the atmosphere around; it is meant to. Have you ever noticed a ray of sunlight coming through a window into a room, shining on the furniture and showing up a layer of dust? The inner truth shines out like a ray of sunshine and illuminates the dusty places, the weaknesses and the unworthy patches in the lives of those who come within its compass. It makes the effort to illumine the darkness so that something can be done about it. We may feel very cross with the sunshine for showing us the dust, but we do see the dust by the light of the sun and we can then take a duster and clean it up.

It is the same with the illumination that shines out from integrity; it will find out all the false places in you and in those around you who come within its orbit. This is not something that you can learn overnight. It is not something you can learn from a book or from listening to me. I can put the idea into your head but only you, by your acceptance of it into yourself, can make it your note of truth. You may feel totally separated from the ideas that I am giving you here, in which case they would not hold a note of truth for you, although your inner note would recognise the integrity and sincerity with which they are offered.

No one can accept anything without active participation, but we could all with advantage dwell upon the point, that we have this secure note within ourselves. I believe that if we could use this inner note more often we would be spared many unnecessary hurts, humiliations, and disappointments, because that is precisely its function.

Truth will always operate upon its own level. You can never receive truth and transmute it into something that is beyond your capacity. If you read something that is beyond your power to transmute, or if it is beyond your experience, it will make no impression upon you whatsoever and you will not remember it easily. But on the level to which you belong there is an active demonstration of inner truth that is pushing and illuminating so that you might transmute it into some kind of action. As I have said, this demands a complete

65

honesty of purpose in you; it demands a careful analysis of everything that you do in the light of truth. If you were to ask yourself constantly why you were doing the most trivial things, it would be a tremendous revelation. How many things do we do, not because our heart is in them but because convention demands that we should do them? As I have said, truth is not discourteous, so if we are behaving conventionally to promote the comfort and well-being of those around us, that in itself constitutes an effective transmutation of the same truth. But if we are doing something to 'keep up with the Jones'', if we are trying to do something to copy someone else, this is not acceptable in the light of truth. We must accept that everything that we try to do must have its foundation in truth.

So you see that if we start at the beginning and examine the word 'truth' with this kind of attention to detail, we shall discover in ourselves all kinds of falsities that have hitherto been undiscovered. Our heart must be in what we do because we believe sincerely that it is the right thing to do. You may feel that this kind of analysis and self-examination is not necessary on such a trivial level of activity, but unless we are truthful in the small things, how are we going to recognise truth in the greater? If we are meticulous in these small details we shall know that we are attracting towards ourselves the right kind of illumination and direction when we deal with things that we feel are a little beyond our reach.

Everyone knows that when they try to uncover their psychic side it can be infiltrated with all kinds of subconscious interference. Many people hold back from psychic development because of this. 'I don't want anything that is not true', they say. 'How do I know that this is not produced by my own mind?' The answer is that if you want truth and nothing else, you will learn to differentiate. Of course you will get your own thoughts and subconscious infiltration. But you are not using that infiltration with a view to deceive; you are using it as a means of getting through the barrier to the inner reality, the inner truth. If you are constantly aware of that note of truth, it will ring so clearly that you will be able to separate that which belongs to the level of uncertainty from that which belongs to the level of conviction. Those of you that have had experience of true psychic awareness will recognise that there is a distinct difference, on the one hand muffled, confused, and with no sharp edges, and on the other hand so clear that you can say: 'I know that was right. I will not take that back'; you know that it came from spirit. There is a conviction, a clarity that finds a response in the inner note of truth; it rings soundly and it rings in tune, but although we can accept and apply it in the psychic and spiritual spheres, we often fail to use it in an effective way in our everyday lives.

Yet everyone is not meant to be a medium or to be psychic in the sense of being consciously in touch with spirit at all times. There are countless people who are using their psychic mechanism without the least idea that they are doing so. They have an inner purpose, an inner core of truth within them. They will say that they are striving to do God's will, that they pray for direction night and morning. They are releasing by this means their note of truth, their spiritual consciousness that opens them up to an inner illumination that is going to shine from them and illumine the dark places into which circumstances and life will guide them. The note of truth is no respecter of persons, but it can only come to those who are ready to hear it. Being ready to hear it entails no psychic or spiritual training, but it does demand an inner honesty, a sincere desire to be truthful at all times.

Examine what you mean by 'truthful'. Don't just say

that you never knowingly tell a lie. Lies have nothing to do with this kind of truth, except that if we use lies as a means of escape they are a deviation from the inner note and we are not going to hear it so clearly if we indulge in them. But lies are the outward expression of false thinking. They are not contradictions of truth so much as inability to deal with life as we find it, thereby necessitating resorting to lies as a way of escape or of avoiding an uncomfortable situation. You will see by your own personal exploration that this is a very different approach to the inner note of truth, which demands only the desire to do that which is good, that which is in accord with the inner note at all times.

This kind of self-examination is a very uncomfortable awakening. Of course when you get to the other side of life it is even more uncomfortable, because then the falsity and self-deception is as powerful as a physical pain. When you leave the physical body everything that you suffer and enjoy will be felt infinitely more acutely. If you are allowing yourself to be lulled into a sense of false security here on the earth plane by not worrying too much about listening for the note of truth, then sooner or later when you awaken on the other side of life it will be a very unhappy experience; diversion from truth is something that can give you extreme pain. As you develop the note of truth upon the earth plane you will find that to deviate from it, to try to shut out its note, will also give you pain.

Some of the guides will tell you that there is only one real unhappiness and that is to feel out of step with God. Everything else is secondary to this. Walk in step with God and no matter what your circumstances or conditions of life, no matter what your problems, you will not know unhappiness. You will have compassion for the darkness around you but your inner serenity will be unmoved if you are in harmony with God; however you cannot have this harmony with God without the inner reality we call truth. You can only find God by a sincere desire to know and express his will for you. You cannot understand this with your conscious mind, but you can accept that you have this inner pilot that is directing you and assessing the situation at all times.

This pathway of life that you are travelling is fraught with all kinds of diversions. Your spirit has to make choices and it is in the nature of these choices that your note of truth is given the opportunity to exercise itself. You cannot say what you would do in a given circumstance unless you have been confronted by it. There is no virtue in saying that you don't drink or smoke unless you have been in a position where you were longing for one or the other. I am using this as an example. I am not concerned morally with either, because the people who tell you so self-righteously that they don't do this or that cannot possibly have gained any virtue from their abstinence unless they have been in a position of weakness where they have been confronted with the choice between denial on the one hand, and easy access on the other. It is no virtue to go through life without challenge. A spiritual experience will have had no value for you whatsoever if you were not tried and tested by circumstances. Every time you make a victory, every time your strength is sufficient to overcome that which is confronting you, that which is adverse to your progress, you add to your stature, your growth, and your light.

You also add to the note of truth. How often, looking back on this or that situation, have you said: 'If only I had known; if only I had realised that it would lead me into all this unhappiness, confusion and muddle!' Had you been using the note of truth on the level to which it belongs, your note would have said clearly to you: 'Don't go that way; it is no good for you.' There would be a clear

69

direction. Think of the things to which you have a violent aversion. You recoil from them because the knowledge that they are not for you is so closely woven into you that there is no mistaking it. 'I couldn't do this', you say, or 'I couldn't eat that'. The note of truth will give you just such a clear direction in situations and circumstances that are detrimental to your progress, if you will let it. But it does demand a clear self-analysis of purpose. It will not accept all the plausible excuses: 'Well, I would do that if only this were possible', or 'If only he would behave differently then I could behave differently to him.' This holds no water in the examination of the note. It says quite simply: 'Do I go towards this situation or do I find myself recoiling from it?' If the response is not very strong, never mind. Work on it, use it and it will grow stronger. It grows so rapidly that sometimes you will regret exercising it, in that it makes life so violently uncomfortable for you when you try to go against it. But if you nourish it by your earnest desire to explore and activate it, then at those crucial times of choice and decision you will feel 'this is what I must do; this I must not do'. It will be as if a wall is placed between you and the situation if it is wrong for you, and you will find yourself almost leaping out of your body if it is right.

Don't mind being mistaken or unsure. If you want truth more than anything else, you will be protected against your mistakes. For instance, when you find yourself having to make a very important decision, when you are striving to use this note to guide and direct you, and yet you feel only a vague response – if you will say: 'I want only that which is best', and follow that direction – then if you have made a mistake the way will be blocked for you. You will not be able to go ahead, simply because you have sincerely sought this note within yourself by way of protection. It doesn't matter that you are not clearly aware all the time of what it is telling you to do. What matters is that you seek its direction and counsel.

There will be many things in which this will be easy, and many others when you will feel that there is no direction. These are the intermediate stages of spiritual growth, when you are not quite strong enough to leave the last stage behind altogether and therefore feel a little uncertain. But this will not harm your purpose in any way if you refuse to be deflected by it. Acknowledge that something is telling you what to do, and although you cannot hear it clearly, try to go halfway towards what you do hear, because you know that it is there and that you must not go against it. This will save you from all deception, both in your personal relations and in the way people behave towards you.

How should we behave towards people who we feel have this falseness? Do we reject them out of hand? Not at all! But we do acknowledge within ourselves that they are not true, and we must help them by not allowing them to make capital of their weakness. So you would not allow yourself to be imposed upon by such a person, but you would not say to them that they were not dealing with you honestly. You would perhaps gently withdraw from any situation involving them; alternatively you would register that here was someone who was weak and that you have a strength, because without that strength you would have not recognised the weakness. So you may not be required to remove yourself, but rather to share your strength with them, so that they may be enlightened by an inner realisation of their own self-deception.

Always remember that none of this is harsh or hurtful in its declaration. If you are dealing with truth you do not have to be offensive, you do not have to hurt anyone's feelings in the process. It can all be done with the inner light that will shine from you and illumine the person to

71

the degree of their ability to be so illumined. Nor can you be hurt by their treatment of you, since this same inner light is your protection. Nothing can harm you through the light of authentic truth, if you send it out and use the protection it affords.

CHAPTER SEVEN

A SPIRITUAL HOLIDAY

OUR THEME TODAY is like a spiritual holiday, because it brings into better focus the person that you really are. You do not fully understand yourselves. You do not understand your full potential. You are indeed imprisoned in your physical body; and this, to a very great extent, causes you to forget from time to time your own divinity and spiritual splendour. So we are going to forget all the things that chain us to this earth plane. We are going upon a journey that will help us to recognise, even though we cannot truly accept, our true spiritual selves.

When we think about spirituality we are dealing with a consciousness that is at one with God. Everything is expressed in complete joy, harmony, serenity, and tranquillity – all the things that make for this deep inner fulfilment that we know, so dimly in this imprisonment, as happiness. There is no real happiness beyond the confines of this harmonious relationship with God. The splendour that is your real self is that part of yourself, no matter what level of spiritual attainment that you have reached, that is in complete harmony with God. So while we recognise that only part of our consciousness is functioning in this physical experience, we are going to try and bring into this conscious realisation the full sum of our own individuality, in this released splendour of our relationship with God.

One of the first things you are going to recognise and respond to when you are out of the body is a feeling of lightness. Indeed, those of you who are conscious of spiritual experiences during your sleep state will have already experienced this. You will feel as if you are floating upon air, in a way that is not just related to weightlessness but to a sense of utter well-being. 'I have never felt so wonderful,' you will say; 'I have never felt so completely happy.' As you consciously allow yourself to drift into this realisation and experience, you begin to try and identify yourself with what you are now, rather than what you were. And it is only then that you recognise how imprisoned you must have been. This, of course, does not come suddenly. It comes gradually. But contrary to most things you experience through physical expression, where the physical predominates, in this state of release the spiritual predominates. The imprisonment now becomes secondary to the released experience. And so, while you can realise gradually how very small a part of you is manifesting in your earthly existence, the major part of you is still enjoying this new-found freedom that is the outcome of your release.

You can register this is many different ways. First of all, you are aware of this state of well being, and of lightness. As you become fully conscious of the world around you, you take in trees and flowers, because you are still, in this newly awakened state, dependent upon physical memories of expressions and beauty. But you do not register them in the limited fashion that was experienced by you during your physical state. Those of you who have this faculty will remember the odd occasion when you did, indeed, feel in harmony and complete at-one-ment with the trees and the fields and the flowers around you. But you will

74

acknowledge that these moments of ecstasy were extremely rare. You had no real understanding as to why they should occur at one time and not another. But here, in this newly awakened spiritual state, you find yourself in complete harmony with the registering of this beauty. In your physically imprisoned state you would recognise in this beauty something that you can only describe as hunger. In this spiritual state of release you are able to go out to meet the beauty and the beauty comes back; so that there is a unifying of yourself with everything in which you are taking part. How beautiful is the renewed joy and upliftment in a way that you could not possibly experience through the imprisonment of your spirit in the body.

Even now you are not wholly free of this imprisonment that has been part of your physical experience. But in this newly released state you are not yet even aware of those prison bars that are far less solid, clumsy, and inhibiting than the ones we have so recently left. But, nonetheless, we are not completely free from these things.

Mystics, of course, describe the journey of the soul as three separate journeys to what are called inner kingdoms.

We have the outer one, which is the physical. It is experiencing and expressing itself in a very coarse manifestation of spiritual expression. Everything that a spirit tries to be and do is slowed down by the heaviness of the chains that represent a physical experience. So it is really impossible to perceive the light of understanding and harmony that the released spirit is going to experience.

Then there is an inner kingdom, the intermediary stage that is the released and awakening consciousness. You only become aware of the chains in this state of existence when you become aware that you are no longer dependent upon a physical experience. Awakening to the realisation of its limitations is comparable with your physical experience except that everything is now accentuated so that you feel your separation from God; you feel your imprisonment much more acutely. This inner kingdom, then, is a stepping stone, a kind of rehabilitation centre whereby you come to the full understanding of your spiritual state, not in relation to each other, but to the job that you have made in your imprisoned physical journey. So, while you are still in a state of imprisonment, your splendour now is acutely accentuated in the realisation of what you can become – because in this realisation you acknowledge the wholeness of your spiritual experience. But you cannot become the diamond that you are meant to be until you have eradicated the bars of imprisonment that are separating you from this full realisation. You are now in a state where you are able to see through a window into the garden, the Kingdom to which you belong, but you are powerless, until you have earned the right, to enter therein.

Let us assume that through varying degrees of experience, you have prepared and purified yourself where you now stand upon the threshold of the third and essentially perfect inner kingdom – the full realisation. This is indeed a moment of complete fulfilment in every sense of the word. Imprisoned as you are in this mortal state of physical consciousness there are no words to describe what it holds for you. Nonetheless, as I said in the beginning, we are going upon an imaginative journey of spiritual freedom. Therefore, although they are totally inadequate, we will try to find terms of reference and comparison with which you might have some glimmering, some understanding, of what lies ahead of you. It is in this purification and restoration to the heart of God that the whole meaning, not only of this most recent physical experience, but of all the experiences that you have had in the past, comes into the full focus of your understanding. You will begin, now, in this state of full realisation to recognise what it was all about.

You do not recognise these as incidents – the person you married happily or unhappily, the kind of home environment, your mother, your father – you have passed through that stage of detailed memory, you have lost the significance of the experience itself in the profundity of that which you have been seeking by that experience. It is the fulfilment of what it was all about that crystalises the experience itself.

It is very difficult to find terms by which this may be made clear to you. But if you can consider in abstract the results of things that have happened to you rather than the things themselves, and try in your own way to reduce that to a feeling or experience, you will have some idea of what I am trying to explain. In this finer inner kingdom you have now lost the imperfections that separated you from the heart of God in the acquisition of this further facet of the diamond, which is your whole.

So you come now into the full beauty of this realisation. This not only affects you much more acutely than anything you can possibly comprehend, but it draws towards you all the other diamonds at the level to which you belong.

So you have this blazing light and glory and everything that goes with it, relative to your particular level.

'What is it like?' you say; 'Is it just an existence that is bound wholly with the experience of ecstasy, that is wordless and deedless?' Not at all. But it has to be experienced in manifestations of activity that are quite divorced from your physical experience. It has no bearing or contact whatsoever with the world as you know it. The most beautiful thing that you can comprehend in a physical state of consciousness would be dimmed completely by the light of this full realisation of complete freedom from all imprisonment.

This, then, is the real splendour that is you. This, then, is that goal, that light, towards which we are all, in our various ways, gravitating. We are drawn, irresistibly, through all these physical experiences and times of bondage, by the manifestation of that light to which we belong, and are inseparable from, in our spiritual state.

You are born into a spiritual group or family that is eternal. This is the light or the wavelength to which you belong. You must earn the right to progress on that wavelength. As you so progress, so your light becomes brighter and your spiritual family becomes closer in this journey towards you. The light itself will always uphold you. It will always penetrate the darkness of your imprisonment and the suffering to which your ignorance and inexperience subjects you. It will always provide you with the illumination that is necessary for you, however dark the path, to take the next step upon your journey. So that, while we must acknowledge the imprisonment, and while we can hope and look forward to the splendour that is ourselves, we must, by the acceptance of both, also accept that this imprisonment, in this sense, is self-imposed. It is self-imposed because of the advancement and increasing splendour that such experience is going to afford us.

This is an important point. When we think about imprisonment, we think of something that we have done to deserve it. We say that we are imprisoned by our selfishness, by our greed, or by our ignorance. This is, to a certain extent, true. But it is not the primary motive of this voluntary imprisonment of the splendour which is the real self. This is why I want you to think and to dwell on the splendour that is yourself.

Now you say: 'Surely this must be to the degree of one's own advancement. It's all very well for these highly evolved spirits who come in this blazing light and glory to talk to us about progression, but look at the long way we have to come. Look at the long way we have to travel.' In the first place it may be that the splendour that is you is much greater than you are able to understand in this present imprisonment. But quite beside that, even though you will have to accept when the time comes that your splendour is less, perhaps, than you had hoped, less than those around you, even then this full perfection will have the same level or degree of ecstasy, joy, and happiness for you as for the highly evolved person. Because to the degree of the capacity that you, in your splendid release, are able to comprehend and experience, so perfection, like a fountain of pure clear water, is released into you. Nothing can stop it.

It is exactly the same as doing the best you can with everything that you do on the earth plane. You say, perhaps, that your pathway on the earth plane is a very humble one. Perhaps you are a housewife. Perhaps you hold a very humble position in an office or a shop. But, to the degree that you are able to give the best you can to those circumstances and conditions in which you find yourself, you are making it an act of worship.

We should undertake to do everything as if we are doing it for God, as indeed we are, and by the full giving of ourselves in even these most humble tasks, we are beautifying and enlarging this spiritual capacity for harmonious relationships with Him. We are lessening the physical bonds and increasing the spiritual freedom. But the joy and fulfilment that we experience is dependent entirely upon the level that we give of ourselves. This is why, in this next stage of comprehension and understanding, the first inner kingdom of realisation, the imprisonments are definitely self imposed. They are the results of neglected opportunities and of unfulfilled duties that we have been afforded as part of our spiritual pathway through an earthly experience. Your physical body, while it holds the strongest bondage and prison bars for you, is less harmful in its effect than these spiritually self-imposed prison bars. Your spiritual release will make you aware of them.

We are, after all, on the earth plane, dealing with that kind of imprisonment now. So if we get that kind of imprisonment in its right perspective; if we acknowledge that there is a part of ourselves that is perfect in God; and that the part that is functioning now through this physical experience is a small imperfect part, and we have been given this opportunity to perfect it and add to the quality, power, and splendour of our own diamond which is our spiritual whole; then the physical bondage takes on the same illusory quality as the prison for Peter of old. When, by the power of the spirit, he was led quietly through those gates that solidly imprisoned him, he could not, of course, escape from the imprisonment of the physical limitation. Indeed he was not meant to. To be fully aware of the full splendour that we exercise as our real selves would be a liability. We would be straining at the leash. We should be constantly overcome at the various vicissitudes and the coarseness of the field of experience around us, to such an extent that the experience itself would lose its meaning and purpose, for our own progress. We would be like a light that was shining into the eyes of someone, blinding them rather than illuminating them.

So the lamp and the splendour which is ourselves has to be reduced, slowed down, and transformed into something that can illuminate the dark coarseness of the prison we know as life. But this is not done as a result of imperfections, or of things left undone. It is doing it, as I

80

have explained, to add another facet to the diamond that is ourselves. The diamond may be very small if our progress upon this earth plane has not been great or if our spiritual journey has been brief. But here again, the perfection, no matter how small the diamond, has the same splendour of fulfilment as anything it can experience in its wider and more highly evolved state. It will draw to itself the accumulative light of its own environment as it becomes released, expressed to the fullest capacity of our awareness and our comprehension.

The spirit in its wholeness must have this harmonious blending of the perfect relationship with the God force. You are not just the rather impatient, thoughtless, neglectful person that you think you are. Oh yes, you may be all of those things too, but this is just a small fraction of your spiritual authority functioning through this physical captive experience.

It is not the real you, it is only a small part of you. In that same realisation, you can call upon the light that represents your whole spiritual consciousness and authority to reflect something of this imprisoned splendour that is the real you. Something of its perfection can permeate and illumine, however diffused and reduced by the force of the circumstances that represent this earthly experience. Something of this real you can shine through.

Think of yourself in your happiest moments. Think of those odd, perhaps infrequent experiences in life, when you have been completely released from all the limitations that go to make up the obstructions to your happiness. Think of yourself at that moment when you said that you were completely happy. Think about that as you would think of a point of light coming through a dark curtain, or wall, into a room completely devoid of light. Think of that tiny pin-point of light, and know that that

81

moment of complete happiness is relative to that pin-point of light in the same way that you, in your fullest capacity, are shining behind this small light.

This is why you do not have to dwell too deeply upon your imperfections. Indeed dwelling upon them doesn't do anything about them at all. You can't do anything about the mistakes you made yesterday or last week or last year. You can regret them; you can feel sorry about them. But that surely doesn't make it any better. You can purposefully recognise that this is only a small part of the true splendour that is you. In this full recognition of your imperfections, of that wasted opportunity, and those neglected duties, you can acknowledge that these were things which you ought to have done which you did not do. Or, conversely, you did that which you should not have done. Let it go. Because, in recognising the splendour that is the whole of yourself, you release a light, a strength, a power to yourself. Remember that the major part of yourself is still attached to the spiritual group to which you belong, and is drawing down to your physical self this whole splendour that is you. It is pumping and percolating this power into this dark prison which your spirit is occupying. Each time you acknowledge this, you draw towards you renewed opportunities in which you can, if you attack them and deal with them bravely, expiate on the earthly level all those imperfections and neglected duties.

Your spirit, of course, is timeless. It is not dependent on months and days as a body is. Your prison term must terminate within a certain space of time. You are given a certain range of opportunities from the time you are born until the time your body has to give up its spirit and release it from it physical prison. Because earthly time is important to the temporal physical existence, your spirit can only function within the limit of that time. That is why you pass into spirit with these debts unpaid and these many flaws in this small facet of that particular diamond that is you. But every time you acknowledge: 'I am more than this; I am more than this moment; I am more than this experience and this situation'; you call upon that full splendour that is your own.

Every time you increase the light by the removal of a flaw, you also increase your ability to release more of the splendour that is you, so that you become stronger. That is why you grow by difficulties and tribulations and misunderstandings and humiliations. Not because they are punishments, but because they force the real you to lift yourself up, and to make you recognise your spiritual authority and parentage, in the *true* sense of relationship with God. You pull down the strength that that represents, and defy those prison obstacles that would deny your right to such spiritual perfection.

Those people who are imprisoned by their indulgences of the body are providing for themselves the spiritual prison which that first inner kingdom represents. When the time comes for them to pass on, it will be much more difficult for them to shake off the prison bars of this earthly experience. You cannot hold or cling to things of the earth; you increase the weight of the things that separate you from God. You will not understand this until you have passed into this inner state of consciousness that is the next step of release from the body.

Don't despise the comforts of physical living. I don't mean that at all. But get them in their right perspective. If, by providing yourself with such comforts, you stoop to make the path difficult for one of your fellow travellers, you are indeed providing yourself with a much more severe prison than this earthly body can bind you to. Because the spiritual prison, believe me, is infinitely more difficult to deal with in that it *is* self imposed. The physical

83

body is not self imposed, it is an experience that you have chosen by way of spiritual attainment. But this central kingdom, that we know as the inner separation, represents the imprisonment that you yourself have placed around yourselves by your actions here upon the earth plane. This is why it is so very necessary to face up to life as you find it. To take these things, not as reality, but the illusions that they are, the prison that they are. They have no part in the real you. You don't belong to life as you find it now. This fearful person that you find yourself to be, so afraid of this and that, so very resentful that this is happening to you – that is not the real you. The real you is a beautiful shining light that is part of your relationship with God. It is perfect in its own right, struggling through the darkness of this physical prison that you occupy now, to release to you the vitality that can reduce that same prison to the illusion that it really is. You don't have to worry about the future, you don't have to worry about what is going to happen. If you do, you are reinforcing the concrete of this prison. You are making it thicker and more solid than you need. Recognise that this life is merely an illusion. This inner splendour that is the wholeness of your spirit, can only shine through fractionally to this present experience. This is the real power. This is the reality, this is your relationship with God, the real splendour that you represent.

If you can remind yourself of this every time you become fearful, every time you have needs to be met on this long travelling pathway that is life, you will reduce the power of your prison. More importantly, you will find yourself much freer when you come into this first inner kingdom of spiritual realisation. Those bonds are very much more painful to experience and to release yourself from, not because anyone is striving to punish you, but simply because in the realisation of your own perfection, anything that is imperfect is *acutely* sensitised and thereby made much more important. Just as joy and happiness have no true parallel in your physical consciousness, so, too, unhappiness and pain have no such parallel.

Don't think of wrong-doing in terms of conventional law-abiding terms. Of course, it is important to live to a social standard. One must have laws and governments and national principles. But remember, the essence of all spiritual relationships is the fulfilment of the law of love. And you can simplify this by taking quietly each moment in time and in life as it is offered to you; offering yourself, accepting whatever you find. You will be secure in the knowledge that, however dull and miserable your prison may be, the splendour that is really your own is shining through and operating, and thereby rendering that prison completely illusory by way of obstacle and obstruction.

Life cannot say to you that you cannot do this or that. Only you, by acknowleding imprisonment, can provide your own obstacles. Oh yes, they will be there! There are difficulties for you to deal with: difficult situations, the burden of health, difficult and unforgiving people around you, or misunderstandings to contend with. You may have all of these, but your splendour can shine out through those circumstances, so that in its brilliance the darkness of your prison must be confounded, must be made powerless to obstruct you.

You will find, too, that there are degrees and manifestations of emotional love that are the stepping-stones that lead us to a wider and more unselfish spiritual realisation of what we mean by that term. But you cannot render yourself free of these bonds that you weave for yourself unless you do everything in love. Now this does not mean taking to your bosom every person that you meet in life. But it does mean accepting what life gives you, recognising that when you can't understand, this is

85

not because it does not belong, or is there by accident, but because only the full splendour of your consciousness focused upon it would bring you full understanding.

The crucifixion, you know, was *not* a vicarious atonement. Christ had no intention of taking the sins of the world upon his shoulders by giving of Himself. What He was doing was expressing the splendour and glory of the wholeness of His spirit to the fullest extent of the imprisonment of the physical experience that He had undertaken. And, because of His power and authority in the expression of that love, He took to Himself the darkness and the hate, the greed, the fear, and the selfishness of the community in which He lived. It was the light of His splendour that really gave meaning and purpose to the crucifixion. He did not take anybody's sins upon his shoulders. He expressed so greatly this power of love that all those who were within His orbit were made lighter and stronger and more aware of their own spiritual consciousness.

Here again, we cannot assess the progress each of us makes. You can say: 'I did the best I could for old so and so. You should have seen how I went backwards and forwards trying to give him this help and this understanding and he was as cantankerous and awkward as he ever was.' It is only the pin-point of light of the real you that can manifest in this expression of what you are doing. You cannot see the result of what you do. You have no idea of the effect of it. But you can, to the very best of your ability, acknowledge always with this spiritual partnership, that there is access to all things and that everything has its purpose. Never mind how apparently useless your efforts seem to be. That is not for you to assess. Yours only to say: 'Where is the opportunity? Give me the power. Give me the light to take it to my heart.'

I was once asked by someone who suffered badly with

arthritis how he could cope with the pain. It was so agonising that, at times, he felt like screaming. I pointed out that as an attack started he tensed the muscles, clenched the hands and generally became rigid in an attempt to *attack* the pain. Indeed he hated it, but in so doing he intensified the prison that it represented. 'But,' he asked, 'how else can I meet it? I have to insulate myself against it in order to cope.' My answer was to suggest that he should go to meet the pain saying: 'Pain, you can't hurt me because I have a splendour that can melt everything you can do to me.'

You will find that if you could meet life, and yes, even physical pain, by embracing it, indeed, embracing everything that comes to you, then something that is the splendour that is the real you will be able to shine through, so that even the worst demands of the prison sentence that life represents would be met with far less unhappiness and resistance. You in turn would increase your power to light your life. You cannot fight that which you love, you cannot love that which you fight. The only way is to be aware that this is indeed a prison, an illusory prison nonetheless, and to understand that the splendour that is you is always, always able to conquer. Recognise that you must love everything that comes your way, must allow yourself to be crucified in the cause over and over again, if that is what life demands. In this power and in this authority we begin to understand.

Indeed, all of you are consciously bigger than when you started to read this. You can feel something of your spiritual depth in a way that was not apparent to you when you began. This has nothing to do with my words. It is your spirit acknowledging the joy, the splendour, the glory that is your self. It is telling you to say: 'I don't have to be down there crawling on the ground. I don't have to be a slave to my prison environment. I am free. I am the slender part of God that is functioning here, limited by this physical envelope that is only a small part of the splendour that is truly myself.' Then you are going to say: 'Come on. Everything that you bring me I am ready to receive. Indeed, that is why I have accepted the imprisonment of this earthly experience. You cannot make me unhappy if I myself refuse to be unhappy; you cannot make me discouraged if I refuse to be discouraged, because I accept everything that you offer me in love. Secure in the knowledge that something of my splendour is wrestling with and absorbing some of the darkness that you represent, this prison is something that I can afford to ignore; secure in the knowledge that once I have left it behind I shall go into that inner realisation of the full splendour. Then only will I recognise the glory that is myself, that I have understood so very vaguely while imprisoned here in this body.'

CHAPTER EIGHT

WHAT DO WE MEAN BY SPIRITUAL LOVE?

As I LISTEN to your varying thoughts and conversations which qualifies us from spirit to realise which things you need most to know about, I have noticed how very glibly you use the word love, and how perhaps with little thought you add the word spiritual as if that in some way beautifies and specialises love. Let us think about love itself first of all. If you try and define it you will find that all you do is to express *effects* of love; the feeling that you have for another person, the feeling that you have for something that you enjoy doing, your feeling for what you believe is your particular vocation. You talk of loving God, but you have no idea what that invokes until you have it manifested that loving God is something that makes certain demands upon your life. Therefore you are disturbed by it. Most expressions of your love are reciprocal. You like being with that person because they entertain you, they understand you, they are able to meet your needs in some way. You enjoy doing that because the doing affords you satisfaction. So in physical and emotional realisation of love there is this reciprocal area. If someone rejects your love you would say it has come to an end and you are not going to try there any more. Or finding yourself out of favour with something you had previously enjoyed, you would quite easily, quite equably, cast it off. These are all areas of love with your own particular participation in them. So when we talk about love we are dealing with something widely diverse in emotion and its expression.

As I talked about reciprocal love, I know some of you thought about someone you have loved from afar; you would dearly love to be able to be closer to that person, but because that is not possible or not meant you are quite content, perhaps, to pray for that person and send goodwill in thought. Here we have the beginning of what I am going to call spiritual release. As soon as you enter into this area of love, regard, affection, without the need of reciprocation you are moving out of the confines of physical limitation. Now in the spirit world you cannot meet with any one with whom you have no degree of harmony, you cannot be associated with anyone there whom you do not love. Love in the spiritual sense represents the level of harmonious participation to which you, in your own state or degree of progression, are entitled. In the spirit world, therefore, like attracts like in a very positive way. Before you begin to sense the Elysian field that this represents, remember, or try to imagine a group of completely selfish people surrounded by others equally selfish. Here you have love that has been distorted, that has been misused, and which is a love of self and those in this spiritual state are now associating with others like them who have loved themselves. Anything, therefore, that you love, or is important to you to the exclusion of spiritual influence, is a particularly unhappy state to be in when you reach our side of life. But it in no way contradicts the power of love. So we come back now to our definition of love. I have said that when it begins to merge upon the selfless, concerns itself with the well-being of the other person, or with improved conditions of society, or perhaps the renouncing of something to the benefit of somebody else, when it enters this area of self-forgetfulness it begins to open itself to the radiation and emanations of power that we now begin to recognise as spiritual love.

I am sure we have no one here who is so occupied with self and all that this means, that they have not sometime concerned themselves with the well-being and welfare of other persons. So for the purpose of our discussion, we are going to assume that you are equally seeking the understanding of spiritual love. Now we have got to separate this out a little for the definition is very much dependent on the point of progress that you have reached. Here we find your earthly experience, your earthly life, is tailored to meet the degree of spiritual love of which you are capable. It will, of course, demand from you a certain reaching out. You come back here equipped with the level or degree of spiritual love that you have already acquired in previous incarnations. But that same degree or capacity for love is now going to be confronted by opportunities, earthly opportunities, physical experiences whereby this spiritual love may be increased.

When you come over to our side of life it is not a question of whether you have done this or not done that, of what you have omitted or neglected, it is in the last analysis an overall assessment of the level of joy. Now this is very difficult to translate into physical terms because, you see, there is no good or bad in the spiritual existence on the level of the awakening to which we are referring. There is only an infinite desolation of what we are going to call separation. You are not aware of it in that you have neglected someone, or that you have turned your back upon an opportunity, you are only aware of it in a terrible aching void within yourself that cannot be assuaged because there is nothing other than the pain of the awareness of it. I want you to bear this in mind because if you try to translate it on to a physical level you will so cultivate an awareness within you that you will be able to highlight immediately any neglect, or opportunity that is being lost in your earthly pattern. You see, spiritual love as such is something that must permeate the whole of your life, it's not confined to your periods of meditation, it's not confined to those moments of elation in prayer, it's not confined to when you feel most benevolent towards the people around you, when you feel most tolerant, when you feel most concerned or compassionate. It is permeating the whole of your being, and even those thoughts of which you are ashamed have a permeation of the spiritual love of which you are capable of expressing. And what those darker experiences do to your spiritual capacity for love resembles the fog in your cities, providing a kind of opaque screen against the brightness of that which you are able to give out. But, of course, in that clouding or screening of that which you are able to give, you are at the same time diminishing your own capacity to receive that love into yourself. Which brings me to the next step of your spiritual pathway here. Most of you will know that you are not here by accident, that you have yourselves chosen to be here, that the whole mechanism of your daily life, your relations, your position in life, your walk in life in terms of your profession, your ability – all these are the tools by which your spirit is able to operate its purpose. That purpose is to increase your capacity for spiritual love. Because spiritual love is a whole divine acceptance of things, as they are, and a recognition in that acceptance of the power within oneself to alleviate, to help, to try to bring about improvement through its own emanation. Now it can only do that by reflecting it through its own activity in life, so that what you do in life is an expression of your spiritual love, unless you are doing it with, let us say, a bad heart. So you see how important it is to understand that spiritual love, in a sense, is the absolute apex of your objective.

When you come here to us the only thing that is going to cause you pain is this neglect, or perhaps lost opportunity; but side by side with that will be the increasing capacity for joy in those things in which you have been successful, in which you have been faithful, in which you have been spiritually obedient – these are going to enhance your capacity for joy so much more. It is not a question of reward or punishment as such, and this is why it is so bewildering for you.

Some, when they first arrive here, are steeped with their own orthodoxy, are steeped with their own prejudices and all the bigotry that that means. They look around and they see people whom perhaps they had despised because they didn't go to church, or they didn't do what the self-righteous consider they should have done, and they are amazed when these people very often are revealed to them in a far greater degree of light and spiritual progression than they themselves are able to achieve. They are often very aggrieved. So they have to learn to understand that it is not what you do in this life, it is the love with which you do it. St Paul, of course, put this so beautifully in his so well known chapter in Corinthians; all those virtues that he listed, without love, he said, were nothing. And so it is. Spiritual love is not an emotion, it's not a feeling, it's an emanation, it's a quality that permeates everything that you do. In that same love it accepts you, as you are; it doesn't demand any standards of behaviour from you that you are unequal to contributing; it says that life is your tutor, life is geared to that spiritual supervision whereby you are afforded opportunities, whereby patient and obedient exercising of the opportunities presented, your love, your capacity for love, will grow. Everything in spiritual law demands contribution, it demands transmutation, it demands something effective. So you have to start by accepting yourself entirely as you are. 'Because I believe this, I must do that.' It doesn't mean, of course, that you go about with a sanctimonious air, and that you've got to pretend that you love everything with which you are surrounded. On the contrary.

Spiritual love has a degree of righteous anger, it can get very angry on behalf of the other person, but it is not allowed to get angry on its own behalf because love, in the spiritual sense, is contributory on all levels; it is by its contribution that the love itself is fed. The more you give out, the more you receive. You ask, of course, for help in this, and you ask for assistance very properly, because there are areas now of energy and authority to which you are entitled, which demand a conscious need to recognise that entitlement. But you don't have to ask for love; you've already got it, you're composed of it; you are born, and spiritually designed, in love. That may be a very small particle in you in your own estimation, but one of the greatest joys in our spirit world, when you have shaken off the throes of your earthly existence, is to lead you into the spiritual sphere of revelation that you are entitled to occupy, entitled to enjoy. You are much, much more than the limitation of your physical body, and you have access to boundless love on the level of your need both to absorb and release it, but you cannot open yourself and receive it on your own behalf like that. By recognising that you are here to fulfil certain needs, to meet certain demands, to occupy certain places in life, and that you are endowed with all the qualities needed to do so, and by your dedicated approach to that particular objective, all those gates of spiritual love are open for you to receive. You don't do anything by yourself when you do it in the light

94

of the truth, the conviction, the positive belief with which you are able to carry it out.

So again, spiritual love is not a thing that we have, or we haven't got. It is something from which you can never be separate. Whether you believe in the life hereafter or whether you believe in nothing at all, makes no difference to the reality of your present existence. You are here. That is real. You are functioning, you are thinking, there are certain occasions, happenings, in your life that you cannot deny are contradictory to the limitations of the world around you. All these things are realities, they are tangible, you can see them, you can feel them, you know them. Spiritual love, of course, has no such affirmation in such realistic terms. It has to be a reflection that is permeating through all your activities.

Now I would ask you to consider how to define love. How would you describe love to yourself? Find yourself a positive definition of your own, think about love in its effect upon you; you love this person, you love that particular activity. Start, you've got to start, on your platform of physical reality, because your conscious mind can only respond to its own footsteps of logic and reason. So why do I love that person? Again you will find, nine times out of ten, in this kind of analysis, the recipient of your love is someone who responds to you; you feel understood, you get on well together. Again, pursue your analysis of love. Examine now the things that are more or less a necessity in your life, and just examine your own attitude of mind as you do them. You may be one of those people who are doing a job that you heartily dislike, but somebody is very dependent upon the material advantage this affords you. It could cause a great deal of hardship if you turned your back on that particular situation. Now listening to me you could say: 'But I'm doing that with very bad grace, I don't like it at all', and I would immediately answer: 'But you are not doing it for you, you are doing it for that other person who you know would suffer if you didn't do it.' That is love; that is love. And here, if you pursue your own pathway, you will see windows, perhaps little small unidentified ignored windows, of love, that you are operating on your own behalf quite unconsciously, because you are doing something faithfully, you are doing something, albeit not very happily because there are many other things you would rather be doing. But you are doing that because somebody else needs what you have to give, and that's the operative word.

Let us take the opposite end of the scale. You are doing this because that's the only way to get on in life, if you don't submit to this one, if you don't obey the rules, if you don't make the right sort of answers and responses, you are not going to get anywhere in life. This has no spiritual renewal, in the way the other example has spiritual renewal. You may feel that nothing matters, nobody cares, it doesn't matter whether you do this or whether you do that, but I assure you it does. You are a unit in an enormous whole, and you are drawing to yourself a greater degree of spiritual power by your behaviour here upon the earth. Although, as I've already explained, you may be acting with what you would call a bad heart, if I were to say to you: 'Give it up then,' you would reply: 'I can't do that, my wife, my mother, my children, would suffer; I couldn't possibly do that.' That, again I remind you, is love. And because you are doing that, the more love comes in, and so you grow; you grow in spiritual love.

We sometimes say of people that they mellow as they get older. This, of course, is because the apparent friction, abrasiveness, of material life is perhaps less demanding on a physical level, but again they cannot mellow unless they have used that abrasiveness, that harshness of life to enlarge the window. They have done what was necessary because this or that person needed it in some way, and this has increased the spiritual love and the mellowness. And perhaps their greater degree of tolerance and understanding brings the increasing spiritual capacity for loving that they have been able to acquire.

So again let us look at the person whom you are. How do you equate yourself with spiritual love in the way I've tried to describe it? I'll guarantee you'll come out of this very, very much better than you yourself would assess on your own behalf. You will talk about your impatience here, you will talk about the irritability there, you will describe all kinds of negative shortcomings in yourself, but the important thing is that you keep on, you don't stop. Of course you could do it more kindly, of course you could perhaps be a little more patient, less intolerant, of course you could; but this is the best that you can do at this moment, and because it is the best, a greater degree of spiritual love is being added to your quota, to your opportunity to expand. And so you would say of yourself you are not nearly so irritable as you used to be; you do not get nearly so bad-tempered. Of course you don't, because you are widening your window.

Go along that pathway of self-analysis honestly but don't get mixed up with self-righteousness, complacency, with separating yourself from the physical material world, and believing that by so doing you are clothing yourself in piety and spiritual progression. Life is meant to be lived, and if God wants you in the market places, if he wants you in the taverns, if he wants you in the house of industry, that's where you will be; that is in no way a deprivation of your capacity both to give and receive spiritual love. But it is not something you feel, it is something you are and it is not something you possess, it is something you give, and the more you give the more it pours into you. And this realisation gives you a wonderful sense of freedom because it always accepts you as you are.

Bring this analogy back to an earthly level, I believe it was Shakespeare who talked about love not being love if it alters when it alteration finds. If that person upon whom you've poured your love, your regard, disappoints you, lets you down, betrays you in any way, it's very hard, isn't it, to continue to love that person? When you can do so, you are surmounting the personal reciprocal area of love on a purely emotional level, because here what you shared can frequently be totally protected against the betrayal or corruption that seems to have spoiled your relationship in the physical world. In spiritual terms you could never be separate from someone whom you have loved in the spiritual way, and loving someone in a spiritual way in no way means a separation from sexual relationships, but it has nothing to do with physical contacts whatsoever. It is a spirit-to-spirit encounter, and as a spirit-to-spirit encounter it will survive all circumstances, all conditions, all the apparent contradictions and destruction that the earthly life can offer it. You will find when you come into your spiritual home again, that those whom you have loved and shared love with in this way are the persons whom you have loved on the highest note of your recognition of spiritual love, because the physical activity cannot destroy that spiritual participation. So you have this predominant factor of survival in all that matters in your daily life. Equally, life may cruelly separate you either by death, or perhaps by circumstance that takes someone whom you love across the world; again, no separation; you can never be separate from people with whom you share this spiritual love. You can so attune your mind and your thought that you can be united instantly. Most of you know that when your body is asleep you visit those spiritual homes where those dear to you exist but again you only meet with those with whom you have this spiritual affinity. You cannot possibly associate in a spiritual world with anything that is in any way discordant, and this harmony corresponds, of course, with the level of your progression. You are not going straight into spheres of light and glory, you're gradually going to become accommodated to the realisation of your own harmony. This, of course, will offer you all sorts of opportunities whereby you can shed the various clusters of things that separate you from that overall joy; all this is taken care off in that same love. There are no short cuts to this release from desolation; nonetheless, everything is afforded you in love by those who are spiritually attuned to you, to provide you with obvious opportunities where reparation can be made.

So there's nothing to fear in this life from any kind of obstruction, any kind of circumstance; you cannot, in spiritual love, be a victim of any injustice; you cannot, in spiritual love, be burdened with something beyond your capacity to carry. In these refinements, because that's what they are, the more you are asked to give the more you are able to receive. So by the same question, then, if you consider yourself to be hardly used, if you consider yourself to be burdened unduly it is because your capacity to give is on that level of generosity whereby in such circumstances you are pouring out something which in turn is adding to your stature. You cannot give out and not receive. This is not dependent in any way upon your request for such renewal, it is dependent only upon pouring out in that way. Then as soon as you are emptied, so are you filled. Do you remember the lovely parable about the cruse of oil, and how as fast as the oil was poured out, more took its place? Spiritual love is like that,

99

and it accepts you as you are, it doesn't ask you for any purification, it doesn't ask you for any preparation by way of purging yourself of this, denying yourself that, because it accepts the level of harmony to which you yourself are entitled. If that in any way offends the standards of people around you, that is not your responsibility. Your only responsibility is to recognise that if life is demanding this from you, it is in some way contributing through your spiritual activity to certain circumstances and conditions to which you yourself have already agreed so to subscribe. Your responsibility lies in acceptance and obedience to where life is taking you – good, bad or indifferent – and dealing with it to the best of your capacity, bearing with your own shortcomings. All these things are part of the dross that the love will gradually refine away, melt away, from all that lies in your pathway.

Don't just think about these words as words, consider them and look at yourself, look at your capacity for love. Don't worry that you are one of those people who can't feel things intensely; you're not demonstrative, you're not effusive, you can't make pretty speeches; none of these things are important. What is important is that you are the person you really are, that you look at life as a positive way of equipping you, through which your spirit is functioning to achieve what it has come back here to achieve, to increase your capacity for spiritual love. You can only apply yourself to the opportunities that life provides, dealing with these positively, recognising that the only true guidance you have is that note of harmony within yourself, that note of truth. I could offer you all sorts of easy ways out, but your note of truth would say: 'I can't do that, that would mean letting somebody down.' By this obedience, life itself is compelled to obey your finalising of these matters. When it's no longer necessary for you to do this, or to be there, it will show you clearly

100

that there is no longer any need for it. And so you learn. But the important thing is that you don't have to feel it, you don't have to acquire it, you don't have to work for it in any specific way. Be yourself, accept yourself in your own spiritual generosity, giving as much as you can give from your capacity to do so, recognising that what you have to give is important to those to whom you are able to give it, and confident that the more you spend the more is returned to you.

CHAPTER NINE

GOD

GOD IS IN EVERYTHING, and, of course much more importantly, in you. I want you to think for a few moments how you would define your personal relationship with God. The tendency when challenged by such questions is to resort to some written philosophy or bible text or something that has been fed to you externally. Indeed we have been indoctrinated by suggestions of levels of understanding compatible with the society and conditions in which we live.

So let us begin together by formulating what we mean by our fellowship with God. Many of you feel it is somewhat blasphemous to try and identify so wholly and completely with God within you that you are no longer a separate part, that you do not have to reach out there but rather allow it to flow and envelop from within. Immediately you are overwhelmed by a sense of awe, a sense of total unworthiness, and this offends much of the indoctrination received through the years. Spiritual law teaches you that you cannot die. It lays great stress upon the comfort of that reality in bereavement. It shows that there is an area of fellowship and spiritual unity from which nothing can separate you, from which nothing can tear you apart. Given that reverence, given that release from the limitation of physical density, there is a lifting of the spirit and heart that can reunite you with those you have loved and lost in a positively, convincing, wholly comforting and satisfying way. You know this as a personal experience, because you know it through the sweet intimacy of knowledge of those you have loved. No one can deceive you about your husband, your mother, your father, your friend whom you miss so sadly in a physical sense. Into this lovely silence of reunion, there is unmistakable experience of renewed love and fellowship. And yet we question that same sweet loving fellowship and reality when we think about God.

Every sweet human relationship has become sweet and loving because spirit has recognised God in spirit. You have found all that is good and beautiful in those you have loved albeit this involves no indifference to, or neglect of, the shortcomings and imperfections which we know we all possess. But love transcends that. They have only to smile. They have only to bring again that loving presence of all that they are to you, for all those negative imperfections to be forgotten; for the hurts to be healed. This is God in them that you have loved and God in you that has brought about this fellowship of united hearts.

Can we not, then, go a little step further? Can we not say all that is good and beautiful in me is the God within me, and all that I have to do is to acknowledge that presence at all times and in all circumstances, to be aware of its power and its strength? You cannot have its power and its efficacy without its reality. If you separate yourself in any way by any kind of 'if' or 'but', its efficacy is diluted. It is dispersed and you will find blank spaces in your life. Now we tend again, as we take a step further, to relate our awareness of God within us, with those things which we feel we should foster in our hearts. We can't talk about our bad temper and at the same time think about

103

God within us. We can talk about our sincere effort to try to do better, and think about God within us and here in these very separations we dilute, we weaken the power. Every time we think about God within us in this positive way we are bringing a tremendous light, that is within ourselves, to the surface.

Have you, I wonder, had the experience of reading something spiritual and finding that it had absolutely no message for you? It didn't mean anything at all. You suppose somebody understood it but you didn't. And then you come back to that same passage perhaps after five or six years. The time is unimportant. You came back, but now you are a different person because something through the years has brought to the surface of your consciousness a greater understanding, a greater recognition. And so now you read it and you say: 'Of course; this is beautiful. This is wonderful.' You might even question how you could have been so stupid all those years ago. Life is a constant tutor in this way. But life is a little different from our choice of literature; it is compulsory. Life shows you by its experiences what is necessary to be either strengthened or dispersed within yourself. It is meticulously balanced in cause and effect. It does not concern itself only with your own progression. Progression is quite simply the releasing of a greater power of God within you. Every time you acknowledge God's unity you acknowledge a greater light. And every time you acknowledge a greater light, life is compelled to find a means by which you can express that light. You cannot express that light on your own behalf. You can only express it by attracting something within somebody else through this extended light of God within you, by tapping a slumbering, sleeping light of God in someone else. And that awakens something in them. Now when we do this by way of influence and example we very often

104

awaken in the recipient a sense of rebuff, a sense of jealousy; most certainly it is a discordant, inharmonious note. But here, you see, you have the power of God working in you on behalf of the other person, and within yourself only a loving acknowledgment that you have awakened something in them that will soon be equally productive. You cannot, then, awaken this power within yourself without affecting and changing the pattern of your lives.

You are thinking – I'm sure you are – 'That's all very well. I'd gladly change my life if I could. But I am powerless. I'm quite helpless to do anything about it.' Yes, we are taught to suffer, not exactly with joy, but certainly with the understanding that we are not suffering unnecessarily. Spiritual law says that you needn't suffer at all, as such. What you do is to use a greater capacity of love to assist you in demonstrating what this pain, or what this tribulation, or what this difficulty, is presenting. If I could, perhaps, take one of you and say: 'I have tremendous pride in your achievements. I know that you have a highly developed sense of courage, of tenacity. I know that having set your hand to the plough you will not deviate. That comes from you as a light. And I have someone here with whom I am very concerned; who is sadly deficient in courage. He has a great deal of sensitivity, and is very much aware of things that hurt and bruise. But he very quickly succumbs to the pressures of life. Now I believe, that if you two people could come together, you could share something of your courage with that other one. You could infuse something of your light into him, with your courage, with your integrity, with your strength. Sometimes, perhaps, you are a little blind to the tender places of life; because you are so strong in your own conviction, sometimes you lose a little of the tenderness that could so easily infiltrate into you. So as

105

you infuse and inject your courage into that one so, perhaps, he can inject a little of his softness, his walking in a little more gentle way. And here is God meeting God in two of his beloved souls. Sharing something which each is in need of.'

Life, of course, is very much more dramatically harsh than that. Frequently it plunges us into situations without warning, apparently without any kind of preparation. But with God with us all the time, there can be no accident. There can be no injustice. There can be no pressurising beyond your endurance. What you are allowing yourselves to do is to become so overcome by the density of life that you lose something of the brilliance that can penetrate into you.

Now the odd thing about God working within you is that it is not the least dependent on your conscious participation now. What God does through you is immutable. Life will persistently provide you with this experience or that because of this immutability. But there are two ways of dealing with this. You can either accept it on the level to which it belongs, and that, of course, is objective in purpose, and use it as a positive means of progression, of constant realisation of how much more light you are possessed of than you realised. 'I didn't think I could do that. I didn't know I had that in me.' This is a simple example. You can use it that way. Or you can be constantly overwhelmed, hiding its brightness of conscious joy by your own self-commiseration, your own constant complaint about the problems and the difficulties and all the negative patterns of life around you. It is your option. You can choose. But it will not stop God functioning through you on the level to which you are entitled.

Let's think about that entitlement. Spiritual law, of course, is quite, quite positively precise in that you have a certain spiritual identity and through various experiences, including many incarnations, you have brought yourself to this point of spiritual recognition. You have if you like, a classification, a hallmark of your own progression from which you can never, never be separated. Who and what you are now in spiritual terms is immutable. You cannot lose what you have already gained. You are the whole of what you have accomplished throughout the area of progression, which is the release of God within you, in all those varying experiences through which you have passed before this particular incarnation, before this particular area of experience now around you. So everything you are is there inside you. Everything you have already achieved is there inside you. This particular experience is part of what or who you are in spiritual terms. But it reaches a further level of identity and of spiritual experience which is going to increase your joy, increase your efficiency, increase your authority. Many of you say to me: 'Oh I have tried so hard to do what you suggested and for a little while I succeeded. For a little while it seemed to be so much better. And then suddenly I was right back to square one. Indeed, I think I'm worse than I was before.' That is quite impossible. Every time you try, every time you make that step forward as a positive contribution to that which God is promoting inside you, you have increased the capacity for him to influence you on a conscious level. It is already there inside you. You cannot be separate from it. But what you are deficient in is a conscious realisation that this is a power, this is an authority that can transcend anything that life can offer because life is subservient to it. Life cannot provide anything that God has not already planned and patterned as a contribution through you on his behalf for the other person. You can't conquer anything, you can't suffer anything, you can't achieve anything without increasing

God's light through you and improving the conditions of those around you. The only negative aspect of that is that with your conscious mind you are not aware of it. And so you discount it.

There is a lovely story told about a primitive man who lived somewhere in America and he was digging over his soil and finding certain hard nuggets with bright metal in it which he just tossed away. One day a mining engineer came along and found this large pile. (You've already guessed it was gold.) He was absolutely staggered at the man's ignorance. 'Do you realise what you've got here?' 'Yes. It's a blessed nuisance. I have to keep digging the soil. It stops this growing and that growing.' He was totally unaware of the riches in his soil. Now the fact that he didn't know its value in no way denied its presence in, or in any way diminished the value of, his land. Only he himself could not enjoy the physical advantages of that. And that is what happens when you deny the knowledge of God within you. But its presence is inseparable. You can't just say: 'God is not with me. He forgot all about me. I don't know anything. We are not speaking.' You can't say that because it is impossible. You can think it, and you can think that it is true. But it won't make it true. And God will continue with the persistent and absolutely invincible strength of the tiny blade of grass that pushes itself through the cement, through the cracks here and there. That crack, of course, represents your need. You say that life is too much for you; it is getting you down and you don't know what to do. But once you acknowledge that life is no longer your master you are already sprouting the strength within you. 'I can do it,' says this voice within you. 'I can deal with this on your behalf.'

What about the tragedies though? What about a lot of things that seem to contradict this whole concept? We think about God in love, in beneficence, in generosity, in

108

all those lovely beautiful things. But God is in the ugliness as well as in the beautiful. How do you deal with God in the ugliness? Of course, here you have a call for the need of fining down the density of that ugliness. It in no way negates the purity and love of God. It is simply that it has become encrusted with all the dirt, the material greed, the selfishness that we know as man's lower self, or his weakness or his density or any term you like to use. But if you recognise that God is in there somewhere, wherever it may be, however encumbered it may be with the density and ugliness which surrounds it, if you refuse to allow anything to separate you from it, you have now an incentive. It makes it all the more necessary now to increase the light in your own experience and activity to deal with that particular situation. Do you get angry about the children of the world being starved? I hope you do. But I hope your anger finds some kind of outlet in asking that inner strength to show you if there is anything you can do. Unite by positive acknowledgment that there are always souls all over the world who are equally angry about it. Link your minds with those who care, not in an ineffective, paralysed, weak, helpless way, but in a positive acclamation that God will not allow this if you band yourselves together in a chorus of His love, in a chorus of His light; that wherever you are, He is with you, in His indignation, in His concern, in His care. Make your prayer a positive affirmation that you can do something together.

Thought, in this sense, transcends obstacles, transcends all the greed and expediency of mankind. That's the kind of power you have. Now do you begin to understand how you can change things? Of course you can change things, if they are the right kind of things, that God is working through you to achieve. 'Ah,' you say, 'that's the tricky one.' 'How do I know I am meant to change this? Perhaps

I'm meant to suffer that. Perhaps I'm meant to endure that.' Only if you allow it to be the victor over you. Does it cause you to be afraid of the future? Does it cause you to feel that you are unequal to meet the demands it is making upon you? Does it cause you to feel that you have not the means within yourself, intellectually, materially, physically to deal with it? Then, yes indeed, you are allowing that extraneous power to be influencing your thought very much more than the God power that is within you. God says to you: 'I have provided this, so that you can see how you may overcome it. If it didn't seem insurmountable how would you know that you could overcome it? You can't overcome it by looking at it on a physical level, because My power is superior to that, and it can only work if it is acknowledged as superior.' So you look at that situation and you say: 'You think you are going to get me down don't you? You think you are going to devour me? You think you are going to make me feel powerless? I don't know with my conscious mind quite how I'm going to deal with you, but I know within myself I have a power. I know I have God within me who is fully conversant with the situation, with what it is going to do to me physically and mentally.' And you can find refuge within yourself.

God also within you has many moods. He's not active all the time. Indeed, on the contrary, many many times He will say to you: 'Come ye apart and rest awhile. I am very conscious of your tiredness. I'm conscious of your discouragement. I'm conscious that just for now you need to be loved. Come, let Me love you. Put your head on My shoulder and rest. We'll face all that life is providing. There is time, but now rest, in the stillness.'

Those who are not so tired, those who are not quite so pressed, are at that moment asking God to use their light, use their power towards those who are weary and

110

oppressed. In this acknowledgment of this time of stillness and love will come to you the bouquet, the perfume of all those who are aware also that God is within them. That God is permeating from them. And you will receive this quiet gentleness. You will receive the most beautiful cloak of loving kindness He is adding to that which has become somewhat run down within your own conscious application.

Sometimes God is joyous. He will laugh with you. He will take those little weaknesses, those things you feel are so dreadful, and He will say: 'Let us laugh at them together. Let us enjoy the humour of it.' He will take your pain and He will say: 'Will you share it with Me?' So that you say: 'I am not alone. I have somebody here with me, to share with. Someone who knows every bit of me, who knows this exquisite torture through which I am going.' I do not mean just physical pain. There are many kinds of pain. There is some anguish that is too deep and poignant for tears. Share it. Let Him take your hand. And every time you do this you send out a light, and that will bring back to you all those who are also in this deep and loving fellowship with God. You become restored to the brotherhood of united recognition of God inseparable within you. Every aspect of your needs, every experience through which you pass, is understood.

'I don't know how to pray,' you say. 'I can't find words.' God says: 'Who needs words? I know what is in your heart. I know how you feel. You don't have to explain yourself to me. I am you. You are Me. Why then do you need words?' This will bring you all that you need by way of freedom.

What or Whom do you mean by God? Take Him from this moment not as something out there, someone to whom you turn when you feel you are on your best behaviour, or someone to whom you have to recite all your shortcomings and ask for forgiveness. Make your God that warm, loving, constant light, a flame of endurance within you which perhaps contracts sometimes, when life tends to overwhelm, but never goes out. And when we can bring ourselves to acknowledge it, we enlarge and infuse the whole of our being and attract those situations to us that are not there to defeat or overwhelm, but are there to show the efficacy of God within us, to show the power of God within us. To deal with those situations, and in dealing with them to enhance His influence, to increase His love, His power in the world around us.

What a wonderful heritage to take into the days that lie ahead. 'I am in the Father, and the Father is in me.' Never to be separate. Taking our lives exactly as they are, saying: 'This time I'm doing it with God. This time it is going to work. This time I'm going to make progress because I am using the whole of my power, not just part of it.' Hold on to that. And every time you falter, every time you feel that life is shutting out this inner joy, just know it is only the night before the day. Just as surely as the day follows the night, this will pass. Nothing has changed. You cannot lose what you already have. You can only add, and every time you try, every time you reach out, you are increasing that power within you. God, then, for you is everything.

You know St Francis held a very beautiful relationship with Leo. I think he loved Leo more than anyone of his brethren because Leo was so human. He was so full of shortcomings. He always, symbolically speaking, reminds me of Peter. Peter, the clumsy, and very, very often weak in his own pattern. So, too, was Leo. One day, after listening to Leo bemoaning all his shortcomings and listing all the things of which he was ashamed, St Francis took his hand and said: 'Dwell not on your

112

weaknesses. Your Father knows your strength and He will not suffer thee to be torn by the cruel thorn or the jagged rock till He has clothed thee with His vestments, shod thy feet with His strength.' God in you will clothe you with His vestments, and shoe your feet with His strength.

CHAPTER TEN

PRAYER AND MEDITATION

SO MANY PEOPLE use these two approaches for spiritual replenishment more or less in the same way. By a little bit of understanding, a little bit of spiritual penetration, we can use both these approaches to spiritual power much more effectively. While they are related, they are completely separate in their effect upon us spiritually.

Let us first of all, then, consider what we mean by prayer. When we pray we almost invariably have a reason for praying. We are praying for something. This may be on behalf of someone else or it may be about our own affairs. But it is most certainly a request.

When we meditate we are allowing our spiritual consciousness to rise and release itself from the prison of the physical barriers and go forth on our behalf for replenishment. This is best done in complete silence. As we enter into this silence it becomes increasingly powerful, so that even our very thoughts are still. We go about this in various ways. For some of us it is as if we were in a quiet wood. We feel that we are underneath trees, that everything about us is still and silent. Gradually all the hubbub and the din that goes on in our mental activity is stilled also, so that we find ourselves at one with this silence. Now this is what I call an

114

unrequested form of strength. It is a retirement rather than a projection. In prayer we project our spiritual consciousness with a specific purpose, and it gains strength from this request, on our behalf. With meditation we retire. We withdraw and release our spiritual energy into something that is unrequested, undesirous, and it makes itself totally at one with this stillness. This brings about its complete restoration. With psychic development, this kind of meditation is unproductive. Just as prayer is a projection, psychic development is a projection of energy and force to stimulate those psychic centres and receive on our behalf such communication that we can translate into something consciously objective. You will see, therefore, that the processes of prayer and psychic development are outgoing, while the processes of meditation are incoming. Now it is by understanding these three processes that we may use all three to our mutual advantage. We can understand the need and the time for prayer. We can understand the need and the time for meditation. And we can understand how to apply the strength derived from both to the fulfilment of our psychic and spiritual development.

So let us think first, then, about prayer. Before we can discuss this, let us look up the definition of prayer. We shall find that it is a supplication to a source, or power, invisible and unknown. And before we can understand truly what we mean by this, we have to acknowledge that there is something or someone to whom we can direct our prayer. So this necessitates a clear, conscious acceptance of another force apart from our ordinary physical consciousness. If you could, in your ordinary physical capacity, reach out and get what you needed, you would not need to resort to prayer. You only exercise the right to pray when you are confronted with a situation which is beyond your normal physical limitations. So first we have to acknowledge that there is something, or someone, to whom we make a request with prayer. We have then to acknowledge an awareness within ourselves in order to understand it. We know that the ordinary thinking mind, which directs us through each day, which tells us to get up in the morning, or to go to work, or to come home and have a meal, is not the mind that we can release in this quest that we call prayer. We know that this is a separate part of ourselves. We are told that people who pray deeply are able to enrich themselves with a tremendous strength and power. We are also told that they are able to cultivate within themselves a wonderful serenity. Now we have to accept that this can only be received on a different level of consciousness from our ordinary physical one. If this is elementary for you, please forgive me, but so many of the things that we accept in ordinary everyday language are difficult to analyse. While you can say that you are quite familiar with prayer and with the results of prayer, to try to define and explain it to someone who does not know the least little bit about it could present you with tremendous difficulties. So forgive me if I rather harp on this definition, this understanding of prayer. We have, then, this consciousness that is separate from our ordinary mind, that acknowledges its accessibility to a power that is normally beyond our reach. We read, and we believe, that all things are wrought by prayer. But we know also by our spiritual experience that nothing is beyond the law. That everything is encompassed by it. So then, if everything can be wrought by prayer, it can only be that prayer releases some aspect of the law that enables us to increase our strength and power. It can increase our ability to deal with a situation or a problem normally beyond our physical ability.

People often ask me if it is necessary to pray verbally. They emphasise that for them it is difficult. They are inarticulate, and cannot phrase what they have to say very well. 'Is it necessary,' they say, 'to ask in words?' But of course, if we are accepting this separate consciousness, this of itself is an answer. We know that that consciousness not only recognises from whence it can receive its strength, its guidance, and its direction, but also knows the reason for this request. So we only ask: 'Do we express this in words?' if we have not understood the full power and direction of the act of prayer. You do not need to voice your thoughts in prayer. You do not need to ask specifically for certain things to be given to you in prayer. All you need to do is to acknowledge that here is something beyond your physical capabilities. In this acknowledgment you know that there is a part of your consciousness that can extend your physical power. It will embrace and take care of the situation that, on the physical level, is beyond you.

Now it may be just as difficult for you to be aware of this in this wordless undefined state. Is it, then, wrong for you to put your plea into words, if you are one of those people who feel that you can pray best by voicing your thoughts? This is *your* release, and it is not important how you approach this process of prayer as long as it is something that can positively convince you that you have access to a power that is beyond your ordinary capacity. This is why we talk about many prayers being purely lip service. If you were to repeat, for instance, the Lord's prayer so mechanically, so without feeling, thought, or concentration that it was a purely surface recitation, then nothing would be accomplished by your prayer. So we have to remember that our heart must be in it. When we do this, whether we do it verbally, or with this consciousness which acknowledges our need and allows a part of ourselves to go out to receive it, so, as we give ourselves to this spiritual exercise, a sphere of light is projected from our aura, which goes out as the prayer goes out. This is why I say if it was merely a recitation, nothing would change aurically, nothing would go out; and therefore nothing would be received.

Let us come back for just a moment to this aura. The aura is the reflection of spiritual energy that your spirit creates as it functions in the physical body. Your spiritual energy supports and supplies your physical body with light. As your term on this earth plane is concluded and this spiritual energy is withdrawn, you would find that the auric light would disappear entirely with the withdrawal of the spirit. It would now transfer itself to the shape that the spirit would be able to form, because it was now vibrating at its own rate. So this auric light, then, is a reflection of your spiritual activity. It vibrates at the rate of your own spiritual attainment. The more spiritually advanced you are, the more your aura is full of light and movement. But in all circumstances, it has for its own protection what we call an edge around it. This edge is a necessary protection against any intrusion upon this sensitive part of yourself that does not have the physical protection of your body. It is opened up when it is necessary to have access to its own source of energy and supply, again vibrating on its own wave length. You can only receive this power into your physical body through your aura. Every time you breathe you take in this life force through your aura. You cannot communicate anything to your physical body except through your aura. So when you are told about people who can draw upon you and deplete you, it means that this firm edge of your aura has been broken, then somebody has access to your aura and is drawing its life and energy from you, instead of you being able to communicate with it and add your own physical well being.

It is important to understand the way this works because it is the basic pattern of what we are trying to describe here as prayer. Now if your spirit, through your aura, wants to pray for something, it has to break this edge. And so it projects itself out onto its own wavelength. It is immediately contacted and acknowledged by all the other spiritual forces that are in your spiritual group. Immediately the nature of your request is made known and everything of a spiritual nature' is infused into your aura, so that your prayer may be met. Let us assume you are in desperate need of a new house or a new job. You pray: 'Dear God, please show me the way. I don't know what to do. I'm absolutely at the end of my tether.' This goes out from you into this light that we know as a spiritual group, and immediately the necessary spiritual forces come back into your aura. So that, if it is the right moment for you to have the job or house, the people who could supply you with them would be attracted towards you at the physical level. Now this again is dependent upon the co-operation of the people on the earth plane who are motivated in your vicinity. So it could be that when you pray, if that person is not ready to meet the demand that spirit is making upon them, they deny this call. For a little while it would seem perhaps that your prayer is not answered. But having made your prayer – always assuming that you are praying for the right thing for your particular purpose – then, if that person doesn't provide it, another person will. Because this power moves around, so that those people who are ready to meet your need on a physical level will be influenced. They won't know that you have prayed about it, or that they have been influenced by prayer. Nonetheless, this is how it works. It goes out through your aura, instantly contacting the strength and the power that you need, and is absorbed back again with increased strength, and increased power, into your aura. This is now emanating from you, and attracts to you, at the physical level, the conditions that are necessary to your particular purpose. You will say: 'You know, it is a wonderful thing. I really prayed, I really did. And the next day I heard about the house, the job.' This is a result of prayer.

Now before we get away from prayer altogether, let us consider the prayer which is not the right prayer for you. Perhaps you are praying desperately that somebody dear to you will get better. It seems a very good thing to pray for, but they do not get better. They pass on, and you say that your prayer was not answered. Of course here we have the same process of prayer. But since you can only draw upon this strength sincerely for your own good and the good of those for whom you pray, your strength and power has now been used to help that soul to let go – to modify, and perhaps shorten, a period of suffering. It is not a prayer unanswered. It is a prayer answered in a way that you had not considered was the right way. So when we pray, we must remember that we will only get the answer to our prayer, if the answer is the right one in accordance with our thinking. We are frequently answered in prayer without recognising the fact, simply because we have a set idea, a set conception of what we want. It may not necessarily be the right one.

Prayer is infallible. It will always meet with a response. You can never pray in vain. You can never pray sincerely without getting an answer. When you think you have been unanswered, it is simply because you have not recognised what has come back. It could be increased strength. Sometimes it does not take away a certain situation from you, but it will increase your power to deal with it, because you are meant to deal with it. It can never disobey the spiritual law or the spiritual purpose on your behalf. It can never influence adversely conditions around you. It must always work for good, both on your behalf and on behalf of those for whom your increased strength is providing an opportunity to serve in some capacity. Your prayer, whether it be for another person or for yourself, is always a knocking on the door, asking for somebody else to co-operate and help. You can never keep this in a small and confined personal compartment. Everything we do sends out rings of emanations that influence the lives of many people around us. Thus our purposes are accomplished.

Now we come to meditation. Prayer is an objective thing – something that can crystalise our need for extension of our strength. But meditation is something a little less obvious. Lots of people get through life without meditation at all. Lots of people, too, would be so very much richer for the experience if they only understood it. Most people that one talks to about this will say, if they are not one of its adherents: 'Oh, but I find it so difficult to keep my mind still. I just can't stop thinking.' These are always the ones who need meditation most. Because everything to do with this spiritual release demands a tremendous amount of self-discipline. Meditation, then, demands primarily self-discipline. We have to acknowledge that there is this spiritual consciousness. We must always acknowledge this first. If this appears repetitious for you, please forgive me. Each time that you are going to do these spiritual exercises you must do them with the full consciousness of what you are bringing into being. So that if you go into meditation by just closing your eyes and trying to still your mind, you are doomed to failure from the beginning. It is not going to work.

First, then, you acknowledge your mind as an active tool for your spirit. You acknowledge that you are withdrawing that life force, that life energy, from these mental activities, and now your spirit is a separate thing from your mind. Do this now while you are listening to me. Listen to me with your mind and now withdraw your

121

consciousness. Make yourself separate. You can hear me but you, the real you, is a little bit away. My voice now sounds very slightly hollow. Now do that a little bit more. Pull yourself away. Now you have separated your consciousness from your mental activity. Keep that state. Now think with that separate spiritual part of your mind. Think silence, think stillness. You can feel it, can't you? There are no thoughts running around in your mind: 'Did I remember to turn off the electricity?'; 'Did I remember to post the letter?' That's all gone. It's separate, it's quite, quite separate. You may have to do this for quite a little while before you get into the rhythm of it. Don't attempt to do what we call deep meditation until you have overcome this outer activity.

Now persist in it and your stillness will deepen. You will find yourself, as it were, in all sorts of states of consciousness, but always the stillness will predominate. There is always silence with meditation. When people tell me that when they meditate they can hear their guides say this, and spirit people say that, I know that they are not truly in a state of meditation. Meditation is a silence. A deep, deep silence. You must consciously approach it in the silence. You can feel this as we talk about it. Now think of yourself as being able to withdraw deeper and deeper and deeper into this silence. It will surround you with a sense of peace and serenity. In the early days you may be aware of certain pictorial impressions. It is not clairvoyance, so don't mistake it for that. But, as you release your consciousness, it provides familiar pictures related to your feeling, so that you can feel yourself in that silence in a quiet wood. In that stillness you recognise a familiar experience that has brought you a similar serenity within yourself.

Now what about the aura while all this is going on? We know about the effect of prayer on the aura. Let us see now what is the effect of meditation upon the aura. The aura ordinarily vibrates and is always moving. As you became more advanced in this separation of meditation, the aura would become quite grey nearest the body and the colours on the outer sealed edge would become intensified and much more solid. Ordinarily we see colours in the aura, so to speak, transparently. As you get this withdrawing to the edge of the aura and this greyness at the centre, nearest to the body, bands of colour around the outer edge of the aura become intensified in their brilliance. It is not like the prayer shooting out. Meditation is an incoming thing. While still retaining its firm edge, the aura absorbs to itself increased bands of various colours, which represent the wavelength, or degree of specific spiritual energy, that we require most. If we required more blue than green, we would find that when this intensification of the edge of colour around our aura first became visible, the blue would be a little less bright, a little less brilliant, than the rest of the colours. As we tapped this outer edge of power, the blue would be the first to be restored. But at the end of our exercise of meditation the bands of colours could be doubled in width, still retaining their brilliance.

This is the difference between what meditation can do for you and what prayer can do for you. While both of them increase your strength, the prayer increases your strength only on the level of your request. You have asked for a solution to a particular problem and you receive the necessary strength and enlightenment that will deal with that problem. With meditation your spirit says: 'I need replenishment, I need help,' and accepts this entry into the silence. By its complete withdrawal, it is accessible to this concentrated participation and purification on its own wavelength. You can only receive to your own capacity. You cannot receive beyond your own strength. But on that level you have quite a wide range. Just as you can never pray without receiving something back, so you can never meditate without increasing your spiritual strength. But remember that, when you do this, life is immediately responsive to your increased strength. It must *immediately* respond with certain conditions and phases of experience allied to your increased growth.

Take your time to understand this, especially if you tend to have a woolly mind which chases all over the place and you can't stop it. Tell yourself: 'That is only my surface mind; my spiritual mind is totally independent.' That is why I say you must acknowledge a separate consciousness before you can get anywhere. When you have done this, accept that physical part of your mind racing about. But your spiritually conscious mind now turns its back on it. Your physical mind hasn't stopped running around, but your spiritual mind has separated itself so that it is no longer aware of its connection to your physical consciousness. So, gradually, you get deeper and deeper into this state of meditation. You come back from the exercise restored, refreshed, replenished, and life immediately says: 'I must obey the spiritual purpose here, this is what I have to do next.'

Can you not realise what a wonderful experience this can be and how very much better fitted we would be for daily life if we really used this exercise? We can use prayer as first aid, as it were. Meditation is a specific process of spiritual application that you cannot hurry. So you must say to yourself: 'I can pray and benefit from prayer at any time, as long as my heart and sincerity are there. But to meditate, I must allow myself time to get into that state of spiritual withdrawal whereby this process of concentrated spiritual thought can be met.' When you do this, you are spiritually restored.

But life must bring you the pattern that is the

responsive outcome of your spiritual strength and unfoldment. You can never, never pray without receiving benefit on the level for which you pray. You can never use meditation without an overall extension of your spiritual capacity. This will reflect instantaneously in your experiences of life. There is no vacuum. As soon as you are spiritually stronger, you are put to work to transmute that strength into service one to the other.

CHAPTER ELEVEN

THE HIDDEN LIGHT

YOU HAVE HEARD me say before that some things we talk about together afford us greater joy than others, and the sense of fellowship and spiritual companionship is intensified when we are able to share together thoughts which, I hope, will release the hidden light within yourselves.

First I want you to accept positively, even if it is only with your intellect, that you are two people. You are a person functioning upon an earthly level, with all its accompanying limitations, and you are another person who has spiritual ascendency over all such limitations. You have a capacity within you to release that second part of your consciousness, and in that release, to experience levels of joy and upliftment hitherto unknown. So I want you to accept as a fact that there are two of you.

Now let us talk about the physical you for a moment. That physical part of you is rather like a tape recorder, in that it responds to all frequencies relative to its own sensitivity and receptivity – it is quite incapable of any kind of originality. It is fed extraneously on an earthly level of communication by suggestion, or it is fed from within, and endeavours to interpret what is so received, in what we call a spiritual sense, albeit sometimes clumsily and erroneously. So the conscious, physical part of you is, then, a kind of automaton. It obeys on the one hand earthly signals and actions, and on the other hand it listens to and tries to understand and apply the inner spiritual signals and guidance. The more you understand this twin consciousness of yourself, the more effectively are you going to be able to operate the much more powerful part of your consciousness that you call your spiritual self.

When we talk about spiritual activity, we sometimes get bogged down by what is known as piety. We feel that spirituality is a denial of all things physical, that anything to do with the physical is absolutely the opposite to a spiritual existence, or level of consciousness. That is why it is very important to accept the physical part of yourself as a vehicle that can and does, when it is necessary, respond to earthly activities, because that is its priority at that particular time. But much more frequently, it is able to receive from an inner power or light those specific directions that go to motivate and direct your physical pathway.

You can, by a proper understanding of your spiritual identity, direct your lives quite positively, changing your lives, and creating conditions and opportunities for yourself relative to your divine purpose. These are facts. The understanding or acceptance of your physical knowledge now, is dependent upon your ability to receive and to operate this wider and much more authoritative level of spiritual identity.

If you will acknowledge as reality this separate spiritual identity, I will try and demonstrate to you how effectively and really purposefully it can dominate your life, and in short, release this hidden splendour in yourselves.

It may appear that I am going to deviate for a while, but I assure you that I am talking about the same thing, when

I say that you are very much more than you appear to be during this present earthly experience. You have had many previous experiences of one form or another, and while these may not necessarily demonstrate any superiority or apparent advancement over your fellow travellers in this particular incarnation, nevertheless you have a reservoir of strength and experience upon which you can draw. This is not necessarily realised in detail, although in certain circumstances it can be, but in the main it is an instinctive awareness. 'I did this,' you will say, 'I don't know what caused me to do it, it was as if something in me told me what to do.' Frequently you are drawing upon this reservoir of inner strength acquired in previous incarnations.

Now this obviously must be connected with your spiritual identity. The spiritual consciousness that we are talking about is an active and verbal consciousness, that can and does talk to you in this inner sense. Sometimes it is called the higher self – it doesn't matter what name you give it – but it is definitely something that does communicate in a positive way with your present physical consciousness. So while the reservoir from previous incarnations is part of that identity, it is not limited to verbal expression in the same way as the nourishment that you received in childhood is not necessarily apparent in your physical ability and prowess as you grow older, although it must be an ingredient of that excellence.

So you are very much more than you recognise in your ordinary, rather limited, physical assessment of yourselves. But much more important than previous experience, is that there is a divine wholeness in you that you can bring to the surface of your mind to illumine, beautify, and strengthen every experience and physical step that you take. If you would always acknowledge to yourself that the physical is the limited part of your consciousness, and that within you is this unlimited power and source of light, guidance, and love – whatever ingredient may be relevant to your particular need at that time – you would find that your whole consciousness would begin to expand.

The difficulty with your conscious mind is that it is always identifying itself with the limitations of earth, because it knows no other way. So it has to be trained into receiving these wider and deeper levels of consciousness, which bear no relation to the limitations, but rather create physical conditions that transcend these same limitations. This happens very often with utmost simplicity.

Ideally, if we could train a little child truly to accept how real is this inner relationship with God, to accept that they have this light and constant support in all that they do, and that anything that is necessary for their well being and happiness is theirs for the asking, then as they grow to adolescence and early adulthood this permeation of spiritual power and ascendency would be second nature, and all those apparent misfits, discords, and unhappinesses that occur so frequently around you would be minimised. This, of course, would depend upon the spiritual level of the child. You know that the child is only a child in the physical sense, the spirit is always adult, so it would depend upon its level of spiritual progression. But ideally this should be part of our natural heritage.

Sadly, however, we are hemmed in by all kinds of teachings and beliefs, that seem to cut across this inner instinctive harmonious spiritual relationship. Gradually we become indoctrinated with all kinds of limitations and obstructions over which we appear to have little or no control. This grows and grows, and in its growth allows ascendency of the physical part of our consciousness to block and to blunt the sparkling and powerful inspiration that would come from within. And then life, because it is geared to try as far as possible to encourage certain spiritual awakenings within us, deals us a particularly hard blow. We find ourselves up against a brick wall and we don't know what to do. And it is, of course, in these situations that sometimes this density of obstruction that has been built up through the years breaks down. As soon as we can allow our consciousness to recognise its own inability to deal with the situation, and ask for help, we have made a crack in that dense wall through which our spirit now begins to percolate and penetrate. When we refuse to allow any circumstances to deter us in what we feel is our particular direction, we are giving increasing power and ascendency to this inner consciousness, that can and will break down the physical resistance.

This resistance does not appear in any challenging sense, it is the resistance of apathy, of misuse, or no use at all. We are simply unaccustomed to dealing with any power outside our own recognisable and emotional limitations. So this inner consciousness is breaking down and educating our physical consciousness to receive these finer notes, these sharper wavelengths, which will penetrate the density of life.

When we do this, we make changes in our auric pattern. The rank materialist has a kind of solid hem around the auric field which is very difficult to penetrate. But when you begin to recognise your own spiritual identity, then you pierce this thick shell, and the light goes outwards. Now life has to obey that light. It will at first, of course, try to obliterate the light in terms of challenge. If we persistently refuse to allow ourselves to be over-whelmed, we will bring about a positive and permanent breaking down of that particular level of density.

Now this is not done by conscious thought alone. It is not done by saying: 'I am spirit here and now, and I am very much more powerful and effective in my spiritual self than I am in my physical self' – however admirable and ueful that may be. The affirmation of itself is insufficient, in that everything around you will appear to contradict it. How can you feel that you are spiritually ascendent over something when you are bowed down with depression, when you are so overwhelmed with the immensity of the tasks that appear to be in front of you, and you have no power on earth with which to deal with them? You don't know how you are going to deal with them. It is very hard, then, to remember that you are spirit and that you have such ascendency.

So having affirmed that you are spirit here and now, you must begin to make sense of your life. Don't think about life as something that is attacking you, or trying to make you unhappy for one reason or another, snatching away from you everything that affords you joy, so that you are almost afraid to be happy in case it is taken from you. You have now to look at life as a positive journey, with a positive objective and purpose. It is supplying your spirit with all you need to enlarge and expand your own spiritual identity, and become more and more the spiritual person that you really are, and less and less the physical person who seems so easily overwhelmed and defeated. You have every reason to welcome the opportunities that life offers, because they are the steps by which your spirit is allowed to grow. In your own growth and ascendency you increase the power, which is the God within you, and make of your life a window through which God's love and light can shine more effectively.

When you begin to reach this level of conscious awareness in a spiritual sense, then you can feel yourself grow taller, and you are very much more at peace with yourself. You are not quarrelling with life, or with people, because everything now has its own particular purpose and objective. Those situations that seemed so incompatible, so out of tune with your personality and all you consider yourself to be, take on a different light now, in that you are now expressing this love that is sweeping away all the discord and disharmony. You are like a doctor who is fully aware of his own diagnosis, and knows exactly how to treat the illness. Life is presenting you with all kinds of darkness, people who are that little step behind, who need the light and the strength of your love to lift them up.

The beautiful thing about spiritual law and understanding is its fellowship and its unity. We cannot grow in light, love, and understanding ourselves, without being of greater service to mankind around us. Our physical minds belittle what we do, but the spirit brooks no such rejection. It says: 'This love, this spiritual light and purpose that is of God, is like the sunshine – it shines everywhere,' and whether people do it consciously or unconsciously, they respond to light, and to all that it means in terms of upliftment. The spirit is not concerned with rejection, in that it just gives, without looking for anything in return. So it says: 'Here is this light and love of which I am possessed – I want to share it everywhere I go. Because I want to share it, I am not concerned whether people are responsive to it or not, because I know that aurically there is no separation or rejection from those who are ready to receive my light. It is only my conscious mind that needs assurance. It is only my physical mind that wants praise, because it is full of doubts and fears and insecurities. But my inner self, my spirit, knows when I have performed something to the best of my ability, when I have poured into it all that I believe in. This demonstration of what I believe is all the joy and serenity that I need.' And gradually, as we grow stronger in our own immunity from hurts and slights, then we begin to feel that there really is a power within us that transcends, and can overcome and obliterate all the darkness around us. This is what we term the hidden splendour within you.

Now every time you bring that joy consciously to the surface of your mind, and in so doing are able to subdue a little more of the physical resistance to its reality and truth, you are educating your consciousness. You expect to be assisted in this or that situation, because God has placed you in those circumstances to fulfil something in His name. Therefore He will equip you with all that is required to perform that task in His name. You are no longer pushed around in darkness and confusion, wondering how on earth you are going to cope with this, or what you are going to do about that – all this becomes less and less intrusive. Now you begin to see the wisdom behind these various experiences, and the scope of opportunity that they afford. How could you have known your ascendency over that situation had you not been obstructed and apparently stopped in your tracks? But now you can laugh at the adventure – you can say: 'I've seen that before, I know how I can overcome it.' So it brings you this wonderful release.

This does not in any way minimise the difficulties of life as such. But if you examine your mental attitude towards difficulties, your attitude of mind towards any kind of situation or experience through which you have passed, you will find that your unhappiness has only been promoted by your inability to deal with it, or to understand it. If you think about the greatest tragedies and problems in your life, you will think of the way you reacted towards them, what they did to you, the person. But take out that sense of injury, hurt, or loss, the sense of overwhelming odds against you, which is your reaction on the purely physical level, and say: 'Because of that I

133

now know that I have a power within me that transcends the seemingly impossible situation. Because of that I am able to forgive to a greater degree, and have more love and compassionate understanding than I would have believed possible.' Then the difficulties are seen as stepping stones, reaching ever further, and causing us to grow taller and much more useful to God, enabling us to make much more use of this our present life.

Your spirit has access to this power at all times, it is only limited by your inability to take it into your consciousness, and to release and demonstrate that hidden and greater power. But the more you educate yourself spiritually, by identifying with this supremacy of strength and power over the physical part of your mind, the greater is your accessability to this wider strength. You will reach a stage of consciousness when you cease to be anxious about problems. 'Nothing can happen to me in this life that God does not want to happen. It doesn't matter whether I stay here a long or short time, because this is merely the vehicle through which my spirit is operating, and if, therefore, my task is finished a little sooner than I expected, then that only means I receive that true spiritual release sooner than I anticipated.'

There is an answer to all your fears – but you have to be honest. It is not a question of telling yourself over and over again until you believe it, because, you see, as you release this spiritual consciousness, then life comes back to ask how sincere you are, and how much you mean it, by giving you yet another difficulty to overcome.

With all this, of course, comes a kind of self-renunciation. As I have said, the hurt and the sting is only taken away if we allow ourselves to be the generators of this love, the donors of this light and strength and understanding to those with whom we are brought into contact. If we are giving, and at the same time expecting people to behave in a certain way, expecting things to be fair and just, then we are, of course, allowing the limitation of the physical to intrude upon this abundance of spiritual light and power.

Now this active participation in your daily life is reasonably self-explanatory, in that you must use all the opportunities that life provides you with, and you must recognise that there are two of you. The physical will on occasions have ascendency, and crush the spiritual part of you. But if you can acknowledge that it did so overwhelm you, without in any way denying the reality of spirit, you will find that those attacks, and the overwhelming defeats, become less and less, and your spirit will grow stronger in its capacity and power to deal with the earthly life.

At the same time, you can cultivate a way of tremendous spiritual release. You will find that as you begin to permeate your physical consciousness with light, conversely it seems to release in you a greater degree of homesickness. I wonder if you understand what I mean by that? There is somehow a hidden pain about this, a kind of longing – something that can be sparked off by music, or a beautiful sunset. There is a peculiar emotional sadness, for which there are no obvious reasons, because the conscious mind cannot reflect factually what this means, but none the less, it cannot be denied. Your spirit is now asking you to receive those periods of joy, of release, that mostly occur in your sleep state.

Now having accepted positively this supremacy over the ordinary everyday activity, I want you to accept now, that with this greater activity, your spirit also requires more conscious restoration. This, of course, will be afforded by meditation and prayer. But you can cultivate a most beautiful experience of receptivity by using much more positively your periods of sleep.

I wonder if you take all your worries and anxieties to

135

bed with you? Try first of all to clear your mind. The day is over – tell yourself there is nothing you can do about it, and always acknowledge your spiritual identity. Put your physically conscious mind to sleep, and give your spiritual consciousness ascendency. Acknowledge that you are going into the spirit world, and are ready to meet with those whom you love, and who love you. You are going to absorb those spiritual experiences into your being, so that you will bring a greater light, strength, and power into your waking thoughts. Your consciousness will receive all necessary enrichment, so that you will be able to use your wings much more effectively.

You can indeed cultivate wings – you can transcend all those limitations, those petty hurts and disappointments. You can bring so much light into your being by really making the most of those spiritual experiences. If the day has been lonely because you have been particularly aware of the physical absence of a dear one, tell yourself that tonight you are going to be together, and you are going to absorb into your spirit the reality of the continuity of love and fellowship that nothing can destroy. If you felt that your strength was not quite sufficient for your needs today, then tonight you are going to ask your spiritual guardians what it is that you are neglecting, or not accomplishing, and you will receive guidance and instruction. If you need an answer to certain questions then tonight take yourself for spiritual counselling, and receive the necessary guidance that will, at the proper time, be released into your conscious situation.

In your sleep you are wholly that wonderful spiritual being that you cannot appreciate within the confines of an earthly body – you can become the person that you really are in spiritual terms. Lift up your spirit and feel it leaving your body and reaching out – free to do what you would really like to do. If you want to sing, or dance, play or paint, give voice to your dreams. It is the fastest cure for insomnia – your body is released from all earthly turmoil and thankfully becomes subdued. That hidden splendour of true identity is within you, and can bring back so much enrichment and power. You will awaken refreshed, and charged with such joy that you can afford to laugh at life.

The lovely thing about all this is that we do not and cannot keep it to ourselves – it radiates. There are people who will say to you: 'I always feel better for talking to you.' Conversely, of course, there will be those who resent your light. It is not a resentment against you personally, but the illumination shows up the shoddiness in their own make-up – this is what God intends. How can we put things right if we don't know that they are there? Inner enlightenment shows up those things that so often we are unwilling to acknowledge within ourselves, and we react to the bearer of that light and feel that we dislike that person. You don't need to be unduly worried that people seem not to want to get very close to you – the people who are well don't need doctors, and you can't walk constantly in the light when your own light is required to illumine the darkness. But you can rejoice in your own freedom from the hurt that that represents, you can feel that wonderful exhilaration of purpose because the divine love has been awakened in someone's heart, and been able to bring it into the light.

So you see, there are endless possibilities here of joyous and wonderfully powerful experiences, things that you have never seen, like someone who has just had their sight made good, and for the first time can see the sky, the trees, and birds; they say: 'I can't understand why people don't stop and stare at these things, to examine them in all their beauty.' Spiritual release is like that – you will say that you did not know that you could experience this, that you had it within you.

137

If you feel this is a pipe dream, my simple answer to you is – try it! You have nothing to lose, and I assure you that there is this hidden splendour within you, and all it requires is a conscious recognition of its power and its potency, to break down the incrustations of physical limitation, that must dissolve and disappear in the efficacy of the divine light and power that is your true identity, that part of God in you that nothing can hide, unless you choose to deny it.

Remember, life is meticulously balanced to demand the whole of your spiritual capacity – it will always push you further than you think you are able to go, because only by so doing are you forced to release this greater power. But if you did it from joy, from expectation of fellowship and a wonderful freedom from limitation, instead of with desperation, heartache, and disappointment, what a difference it could make to your lives! And much more importantly, what a difference your life would make to those around you.

I want you to acknowledge your inheritance, and start now, from this moment. Hold up your head, and know that God has chosen you to walk a path that no one else can travel. He has equipped you with a power, a love, and grace that is never absent, as long as you go inside to receive it, and allow it to penetrate the density of conditions around you. At His bidding, with His will and purpose, those conditions now carry the hallmark of His love, and His dependence upon your obedience to His direction.

CHAPTER TWELVE

THE LIGHT OF THE WORLD

L IGHT IS SURELY the most important factor in our consciousness. In the gospel of St John, Jesus was reported as saying: 'I am the light of the world; he that followeth me shall not walk in darkness, but shall have the light of life.' Inasmuch as He was demonstrating the Christian teaching – Christian in its universal sense, in its capacity for love and direction – of course He would advocate that He was indeed the light of the world, and that those who walked in His pathway, and His footsteps, must be included in that light. But He did not mean to suggest by this that He was the only person who had this faculty of light. On the contrary, every one of you emits a degree of light. Life is so arranged for you that the density of light is contrasted with a degree of darkness which your light is compelled to combat. This is why your circumstances are as they are – not to make things difficult for you, not to make anything impossible for you to achieve or attain, but that your light may be used to illumine the darkness.

Let us think about light. You know that light is brought to the earth by the sun; that the solar systems are obedient to law; that everything to do with light is on a much faster wavelength than darkness. To the degree that we are able

139

to harmonise light, we are able to use it. But all the artificial means we use to assimilate light are inferior when put beside the real thing. Electric light, however bright it may be, cannot be compared with light itself. We accept, then, light and darkness as two opposites of the same pole. We can take the one as a position of attainment, and the other as a means by which we are able to improve that position.

Spirit light is not dependent upon the physical solar system. It is, because of its much faster vibration, infinitely superior to sunlight. Those of you who have had out-of-the-body experiences in the spirit world have all remarked upon the brightness. The clairvoyant sees everything in a brighter light than they are accustomed to on the physical plane. We know that as we progress spiritually, looking from a distance we can see only light, we cannot focus on shapes or forms because the light is too bright for us to gaze upon. To attune ourselves to these rates of vibration demands purification by way of self abnegation. That is a complete rejection of the darkness. Every time that you try to do something that you believe to be right, for whatever reason, you are making a conquest over the darkness. You are increasing your light, and decreasing the darkness, and this is part of the usefulness we have to each other.

If you could reduce this to physical terms, imagine yourself going through a dark tunnel, and someone walking ahead holding a candle. You are comforted by this candle, although you note that it does not illumine the darkness a great deal. It gives you something you can rely upon; you don't feel quite so lost. We are, each one of us, candles to the other. You have someone walking ahead of you with their candle; you in turn are holding a candle so that someone who follows you may walk in the light.

This light is limited to your capacity, your degree of

spiritual attainment. You are born into this world with the spiritual light that you attained for yourself by previous experience. But you have come with the specific purpose of increasing the light, and you have accepted the experience that life provides as the means by which this may be accomplished. Jesus was demonstrating this when He talked about being the light of the world, in that He recognised that He was, what we would term, an advanced spirit. He was closer to the heart of God in His understanding and attainment than it is possible for us to understand; and it was in this at-one-ment with God that the brilliance of His light was made manifest.

This brilliance, of course, limits our capacity to follow His example, in that the light that He carried was almost too bright for those who sought to follow Him, and indeed it has been too bright for us who have come after Him; it was His spiritual attainment. But for each one He provided a canopy of light whereby they could light their own candles of attainment. This is why the Christian testimony is of such great importance to those who have been made aware of it. It is not the whole picture, not the whole truth, but because in Christian countries this example has been made manifest through the ages, it is a very good example of what this spiritual light can achieve in its conquest of the darkness. In His complete self-abnegation, Jesus was enabled to confound the darkness of greed and materialism.

This, of course, was His greatest attainment. In this His light shone most brilliantly, and it was in this victory that the candle of Christianity has been kept alight through the centuries. Not so much in the ministry, but in the resurrection was the light of the world made truly manifest. It provided a meaning, a purpose, a positive assurance of the nearness of God, and the absolute conviction that man was part of God, and God was part of man. It is this light that we bring with us when we come into the physical experience from time to time, and we are expected to use this on behalf of each other to illumine and overcome the darkness.

We use this in many different ways. First let us take those who feel that their lives are restricted and surrounded by all kinds of obstacles, misunderstandings, and disunity. Let us say: 'I believe that I have this light myself. It cannot go back to spirit less than it was when I was born.' This again is demonstrated in Christ's parable of the talents. While the man was very angry with the man who returned to him only the one talent, it was made very clear that he *did* return the one talent. He could not have lost that one talent without attempting to increase it. If that sounds paradoxical, think about it. He could only lose it by making an effort to increase it. Indeed, in the parable it would have been far better for him, in a spiritual sense, if he had lost it, in that it would have shown that he had tried. But he didn't, he buried it in the ground and kept it safe. This is all we can do with the opportunities that life provides – we can multiply the light, we can increase it, or we can bury our potential in the ground. But we cannot become less than we were.

It is better for you, in your efforts to increase this light, however misguided and confused you may be, to make mistakes, rather than to play safe and do nothing. You will never increase your light by inactivity or negativity. You will make mistakes, but quite often in your mistakes you will increase your light. Paradoxical as it sounds, you will do things that you will regret, but the very regret may be the compassion and tolerance that is needed to increase your light as a result of the experience. So you cannot possibly live in the way that you are meant to live without increasing your light.

The trouble is – and Jesus went to great pains to

simplify this – that we are fundamentally much too complicated; we endeavour to find all kinds of reasons why we can't do this or that, and in doing this, we bury our light. We talk glibly about progress and service, and we balk at the first opportunity that is provided. We say that we don't like this person, or we don't want to do that thing, that it is absolutely impossible in the circumstances. These are all means of escape, promoted by the powers of darkness, which works on a much slower vibration, and on the physical level has much easier access to us, to overcome us. We listen to these kind of reasons much more than we realise, and much more than the reasons which belong to the light, because these demand self abnegation, implicit obedience, and complete at-one-ment, with the sure knowledge that we are here specifically to give this same light one to another.

We cannot do without the light that we are following, and the person following us cannot do without the light that we are providing. We are representatives of God in this capacity, so if we recognise this, we can illumine the world in a way that is impossible without our individual acknowledgment of this. If you study the efforts of any member of society who has endeavoured to improve or uplift society, you will see that they have met with all kinds of opposition, obstacles, and difficulties, whereby they could be persuaded to give up the task, and become once more one of the crowd.

Why is it, then, that when we are so dependant upon light, we so persistently reject it? There are two sides to every spiritual advance, in that victory on one side brings defeat to the other; you cannot have spiritual victory, that is the developing of the light, without the conquest of the darkness, or the physical.

The physical has an animation, a life force of its own, and it resists us on the level of the slower vibration to

143

which it belongs. It endeavours to discount the light, to dim it by selfishness, thoughtlessness, material greed, hate, and all the things that are part of the darkness, and opposite to the light. It will persuade us in very plausible terms, that we ought not to be doing this, or we should be doing that. It will tell us that it is no good helping so-and-so, because he is not worth helping; that we are only making it worse in that we are making it too easy for him, and thereby weakening his capacity to overcome his difficulties, and so on. If we will not listen to that kind of argument, it will tell us that we are not physically well enough to do this service, and that we owe it to those around us, and ourselves, to keep fit and well by looking after ourselves, and not overdoing things by taking on that service. It will attack us in all kinds of plausible ways. It will never attack us in a way it knows could not succeed – for instance, if you are an inherently honest person it would never persuade you to steal. But it would try to undermine you in a much more subtle way.

Let us then think about this darkness. It is a very powerful weapon, as witnessed by the complete failure, in the end, of Christ to convince His followers that He was indeed an emissary from God, and as such had nothing but love and spiritual protection to offer them. The darkness overcame the light in the heart of the people, but the light became increased by the complete sacrifice of Jesus. You could say that He was wrong in allowing these people to bring upon themselves the sin of His destruction. But it was in the complete giving of Himself in this way that He lit the light for all eternity for those who come after, by this complete self-renunciation in physical terms. Nobody has ever been asked to do so much. Nothing that could happen in ordinary physical life can compare with this complete abnegation of self as demonstrated by the crucifixion. You can quote many

144

other examples, if you are not a Christian, but I am talking to Christians, and therefore I am using the Christian example as the most familiar one. You see here the arguments carried to their ultimate conclusion. You can say: 'It is no good doing this, I am getting nowhere' – but this is denied in this light. I am the light of the world, and those who come after me will walk in the light. Those who follow my example, those who endeavour to treat their fellow men as brothers, and seek to serve them no matter what the cost, *must* follow me in the light, and, of course, become part of the light themselves. This is the importance of this manifestation of light.

Often we cannot see that this light is giving effective direction and guidance to those who come after us. We can only feel the pressure of circumstances, the heartache, the discouragement, and the sense of futility and failure, and the unending round of drudgery that life represents. Yet every time we apply ourselves physically to the opportunities that life provides, we are increasing the light. It is as simple as that.

We are brought into touch with those whom we can illumine, and in turn with those who can illumine us as we need it. If the light is dimmed by our rebellion this is the responsibility of all of us, since at one time or another we have all failed in our particular contribution. This, of course, is the essence of the atonement. By applying ourselves whole-heartedly, irrespective of the behaviour of those around us, irrespective of the way we appear to be rejected and slighted in that endeavour, if we persist in this, to a certain extent we take upon ourselves the darkness of the sins of those around us.

The atonement is presented through orthodoxy as Jesus' sacrifice for mankind. In His complete acceptance of this darkness of hate that brought about His crucifixion, and in His sincere love and compassion that could petition on behalf of the very people who destroyed Him, He took away some of their darkness, and put in its place some of His light. This is atonement, not dying for your sins as such, but every time somebody still goes on in spite of the difficulties, something of this compassionate love is being exercised and something of the darkness is being absorbed in the light of their lives.

When you go into the spirit world, if you have not lived the right kind of life on earth, you will ultimately be in a place where it is not as light as for those of your loved ones who have perhaps lived a better life. They can voluntarily share their light with you, they can come to you; but you can not go to their place of light because it is too bright for you. They can be with you in your darkness, and in the light of their spiritual love, your darkness is eased.

This is atonement. This is bearing, through love, your sins. It is accessible through light and understanding to all of us. But it also denies us the ability to make excuses. That is why we cannot say: 'If only they would do their part I will do mine.' We can only say: 'Pray God for a greater capacity for loving, so that what is deficient in them, I may make up by my own light of love and understanding.' This, of course, is walking in the light. We can only walk in this kind of light if the person who is emanating it has sufficient love, that we may be given this kind of succour and help. We cannot accept this unless we ourselves are willing to do something about it. And so it goes on.

You know that psychics are recognised by the auric glow that they emit. You will ask: 'What has being psychic to do with spiritual attainment?' It has nothing, but those who are psychic are obviously spiritually separated enough to have recognised the reality of the spirit, so are advanced enough in that sense to be enabled to emit this spiritual glow. They have learned that in a previous experience – they must have done. To the degree that they are able to emit this light, they attract, very often from the astral, people who see that light and attach themselves to it because of the comfort it affords them. Quite often they make the naturally psychic person, who has no knowledge, very uncomfortable, and it is only by applying ourselves to a wider understanding and knowledge through prayer, that we find the direction and the light that we need to solve whatever is perplexing us, or causing our particular darkness.

This light will always attract those who are wandering in the darkness. This is much more apparent in the spirit world than you would accept, but, believe me, the same thing happens here on the earth plane. Those who find your light comforting and helpful are attracted to you. You draw them by this magnetic field that you call the aura, which emanates on a certain wavelength, and registers to those who are attracted to it on a spiritual level. It appears to them as light, and they are drawn from their own darkness into the light. Now if we accept this, we must accept the opportunity that life provides to serve each other. We cannot do without each other, all of us are interdependent.

We are constantly running around in circles, trying to bury our talent, for every kind of reason. You say: 'I am not a good person at all – I fail to see how I could help anybody.' In such circumstances, it may be that you have a very long way to go – we all have. But there is always someone who has still further to go than you, and you can lighten their pathway. You will find too that if you have refused to face a situation, you are brought back to it time and time again in your thoughts. You cannot escape, because you have not fulfilled what it represents. There is no hell as such, but the mental suffering that such situations bring upon us is quite impossible to describe, if we have repudiated life, and refused to acknowledge what life is offering us in order to increase our light, and sooner or later we are going to have to deal with it.

What does it all mean then? It means quite simply that, whether we like it or not, we have an auric emanation that represents light, and we are going to be sent into patches of darkness where our particular light is beneficial and advantageous. This, of course, involves people and situations and conditions of life relevant to that particular manifestation of darkness and light, and it means quite simply that we put our hand into the hand of God, and say that we will accept this opportunity to serve Him, in the knowledge that in so doing, we are endeavouring to increase the light of understanding of these people, these conditions, and these circumstances in which we find ourselves.

It is in this complete acceptance that we recognise the spiritual power that can sustain us. We are independent of the results as such, and we are frequently confused as to why we are there at all, but we can accept that there is a light that is going out from us all the time, and that this light is going into the darkness of these circumstances every moment. Every one of us here is emitting this light. Some lights are brighter than others, and all of us are profiting by the brighter lights, in that some of the brightness is communicating itself, and we are less dim than we would have been without the proximity of that light. It won't stop there. Because we have been made brighter by this proximity, this influence, life will now present us with a greater degree of darkness, so that the more light we become, the more dark we encounter. And the more difficult it can be to understand, unless we resort constantly to the replenishment of our spiritual vitality by prayer and meditation, to maintain the light, and not allow the darkness to overwhelm us.

Every one of us knows the darkness of despair on occasions, but every one of us knows also that we have crept out of this, however bruised and battered in the process. All of us know the darkness of utter futility and discouragement, when we have said: 'I can't go on, I can't bear this another moment.' But we know that we have picked ourselves up and carried on again. Now this seems a very contradiction of this light, and yet the very circumstances that have brought us to our knees are the means of brighter illumination. It doesn't matter if you don't know whether that is the right thing to do. It doesn't matter if you feel that you are being pulled in two directions. Do the best you can with the thing that is nearest to you, and you cannot help but illumine the darkness.

The light of the world means you. Without your light others will stumble. Somebody will fall unless we each do our part. When we pray sincerely for the appeasement of hunger, for peace, for those sick and suffering, we increase the light. There is a kind of pool of light that this type of prayer adds to. Those who work with these distressed souls are strengthened in their efforts to help them by our prayers. It doesn't matter that we don't know them, or they us – we have increased the light, and the light has increased their spiritual strength, so that they have a motivation for good.

This is what light does in a community. It will always help those around you, whether they are aware of it or not. You may say: 'That is all very well! I did this and that, and it was disastrous! I can't see that I did any good at all.' Dear friend, if you did what you believed to be right at that moment, it must increase the light. Hold on to this, and don't be hoodwinked by circumstances and conditions; it is an absolute, immutable law. You are emitting a light here and now, and life is compelled by this to provide you with opportunities by which that light may be increased. You are provided with the talent – it is up to you to multiply it. Whether you do this or not, you cannot lose the light you came here with. You have nothing to lose whatever by trying to give yourself to those opportunities and circumstances as they arise.

It is only when we stop, and say the price is too high, that we limit our capacity for light. Light is increased only by applying ourselves, by whatever means, to the things that are offered to us by way of service. Think carefully about this now. Don't worry about the mistakes, don't worry about the wasted years and time slipping away – there is no such calculation in the spirit world, it is simply a question of now. And in doing to the utmost what life provides, you are both giving and receiving light. If each of us could faithfully fulfil those opportunities as they arise, striving to be obedient to them, seeking to use our knowledge and understanding by way of further enlightenment of what we can do, and how we can do it, not allowing ourselves to be persuaded that inactivity, or a kind of passive resistance is the answer, then we will be shedding this light. *You* are the light of the world, and those who walk after *you*, must indeed walk in the light.